T0365341

MISSION POSSIBLE:
SYNERGISTIC ACADEMICS

Saving U.S. Educational Exceptionalism

ALMEDA M. LAHR-WELL, Ph.D.

To order additional copies of this book, contact:
Xlibris
844-714-8691
www.Xlibris.com
Orders@Xlibris.com

ISBN: Softcover   978-1-6641-3208-5
          Hardcover   978-1-6641-3209-2
          EBook   978-1-6641-3210-8

Library of Congress Control Number: 2020918551

Print information available on the last page

Rev. date: 02/04/2021

CONTENTS

Dedication viii

Acknowledgements ix

Epigraph x

List of Illustrations xi

Forward (Gail Mueller) xii

Preface xiv

Introduction xv

Chapter I   Why Phonics? 1

Chapter II   What Happened? … 400 Years of U.S. Education History 4

Chapter III   A Nation at Risk 10

Chapter IV   Determined to Self-Destruct 15

Chapter V   The Answer to the Tax-Supported Empire … Monopoly 19

Chapter VI   U.S. "Traditional" Education's Moral and Intellectual Bankruptcy 26

Chapter VII   Myth Buster: True or False? More Money=Better Education 36

Chapter VIII   Twenty-First Century NCLB and Much More… 41

Chapter IX   Still A Nation at Risk 52

Chapter X   The Degradation of U.S. History in School Textbooks 58

Chapter XI   Antidote to Common Core … The Lahr-Well Difference 65

Chapter XII   One-Size-Does-Not-Fit-All! 71

Chapter XIII   Here is the Answer: Saving U.S. Educational Exceptionalism! ... 73

Chapter XIV   Myth Buster: True or False? "There's No Place Like" Lahr-Well Academy (of SA) 77

Chapter XV   Conclusion: In Every Life There Are Defining Moments! This is One of Them! 80

Endnotes 85

Works Cited 87

For how many decades have you heard, "Our U.S. Education System is failing our kids"?

How many times have you heard … or have you said, "My district is a 'Cadillac' school district, and my child is a straight A student"?

Then … ask yourself:

How prepared are college and university graduates for the national and/or international job market?

A vast majority of recent graduates say they are "well prepared" for their new jobs. About one-half of U.S. business and industry managers believe this to be true!

Too many of our U.S. college/university graduates cannot:

- put a subject and predicate together
- make change without a computerized cash register
- balance a checkbook
- build a budget
- find the U.S. on a world map
- cite the 1st, 2nd, 15th, or 19th U.S. Amendments

Are these students being **educated** or are they being **indoctrinated**?

In the pages of this book, you will find answers to all of these questions!

Before you enter the pages of this book, I **must** share with you a quote I do not recall having ever read before! Having spent the last 50 years as a public speaker, I have written multitudinous papers and presentations. I wrote my dissertation at the age of 26. However, as I was **dragging** through the 4th proofreading of this 1st book, I **happened** across this quote from Sir Winston Churchill. I must confess that it lifted my spirits as I inched toward the finish line! "Writing a book is an adventure. To begin with it is a toy then an amusement. Then it becomes a mistress, and then it becomes a master, and then it becomes a tyrant and, in the last stage, just as you are about to be reconciled to your servitude, you kill the monster and fling him to the public." Here's to you, Winston!!!

This book gives an answer to the U.S. pre-kindergarten through grade 12 academic crises which are undermining our "American" values, our academic excellence and our U.S. global positioning in the worlds of business, industry, science, technology, and finance.

It begins with a chronological examination of the U.S. American education system from 1635 to today, explaining the benefits, limitations, and damages of new and numerous educational trends, fashions, fads, and dogmas that were supposed to have corrected the education system's deficiencies. It highlights a few of the major critics who exposed the catastrophically declining results, bringing attention to the U.S. students' lack of reading, math, and reasoning skills … thus resulting in millions of children (and adults) being **left behind … lost … without adequate, life-functioning skills!** This has not only put these students individually at risk, but has put our nation at risk … in global business, science, technology, and financial competition.

Synergistic Academics is a curriculum that not only provides individualized, tailored, basic skills curriculum but also weaves together world history with American history, mathematics, language arts, introductions to 5 foreign languages, biology, chemistry, earth science, physics, music appreciation, hands-on art, research and composition, technology, engineering and robotics … **all woven together** into **one** tapestry … for **all** students (pre-kindergarten through grade 12). It offers a **living-breathing, patriotic curriculum** (**proven by** 35 years of nationally-standardized test results) that not only corrects the U.S. educational deficiencies but provides the tools students need to aspire to **American exceptionalism.**

EDUCATION

Ph.D. St. Louis University, St. Louis, MO
Licensed and Registered Financial Representative

HONORS AND AWARDS

Business *Athena Award,* Edwardsville-Glen Carbon Chamber of Commerce
Who's Who in American Education
"Hometown Hero" Glen Carbon, IL
"Outstanding Young Woman of America"
"Outstanding Teacher" University of Illinois

The Unique Contribution

The unique contribution of the book is that it offers a **proven** answer (in the form of a curriculum-for-lease) to the continued decline of "American" moral values, patriotic fervor and educational exceptionalism of the 18th, 19th, and early 20th centuries' U.S. educational environment.

The Intended Reader

- news media that is committed to making a **positive** difference in our society ... a media that **knows professionally** that **one-size-does-not-fit-all**

- news media that sees the value of "disruptive" education

- business leaders who, in order to better-train their own work force, **should be interested in** a U.S. pre-kindergarten through grade 12 educational program that has already provided a foundation of exceptional, academic skills, as well as creative and innovative thinking

- educational leaders who will have an "opened" mind to a program that teaches **every** student ... and who will implement an intensive, comprehensive curriculum that is unmatched in the nation

- parents, clergy, and other moral leaders who will be reinforced by the ethics, religious heritage and patriotic recognition in the curriculum

- college/university presidents **who should be interested in a preparatory school that will produce exceptional, entering, college/university freshmen**

- U.S. military schools ... already in existence ... where those in charge **should be interested in an exceptional program that will produce exceptional graduates**

DEDICATION

I dedicate this book to **my parents Guy and Ruth Lahr** who laid the foundation for my faith life … in my becoming who I am (a disciple of/for Jesus) … and whose I am (a child of God); and to my **husband Ralph** who has stood by me in more than 45 years of marriage … "putting bread on the table" … while I kept giving it away; and to our **daughters Alexia and Arin** … both successful professionals, in their own rights … as well as extremely loving, dedicated mothers … and to their spouses and children … **all** who fill my life with added joy. [And] to **Janice Bown**, retired Ph.D., who mentored me … as a young, female professional … to become the **independent, innovative maverick** I have become.

ACKNOWLEDGEMENTS

It is with indebted gratitude that I express a humble, but profuse thank-you to:

- **Gail Mueller:** retired Master's Degreed teacher; award-winning, master musician; business entrepreneur; friend since childhood … for almost 60 years now … for the dozens and dozens **and dozens** of hours she spent proofing, editing, and offering rewordings to my efforts.

- **Nancy Gaines:** board member Lahr-Well Academy, retired Master's Degreed mental health therapist, Licensed Clinical Professional Counselor, numerous social service agencies and college leadership positions, friend for more than 25 years … for added proofing and offering additional suggestions … "pouring over" the entire manuscript … **numerous** times.

- **Lynn Rogers:** retired Master's Degreed education case worker; truancy interventionist; and guidance counselor; friend for more than 20 years … for her patience through **a great many** title changes … **and** the creativity she brought to the jacket cover design.

EPIGRAPH

"Men occasionally **stumble over the truth**, but most of them pick themselves up and hurry off as if nothing had happened." (Winston Churchill)

LIST OF ILLUSTRATIONS

Illinois Policy Chart: Illinois spending on education per student among highest in the Midwest 21

Illinois Policy Chart: Illinois students trail nation in college readiness 22

Illinois Policy Chart: Virginians enjoy lower total tax burden, lower property tax burden than Illinois. 23

Illinois Policy Chart: Virginia students are better prepared for college than Illinois students 24

Lahr-Well Academy Learning Bar Graph.. 35

Common Core Math (per Donna Hearne) 44

FORWARD (GAIL MUELLER)

I have known Dr. Almeda Lahr-Well since we were in seventh-grade band in junior high school. We both played the clarinet and competed, fiercely, for the first-chair position, yet we became good friends. Yes, her name was always displayed for her straight-A report cards. Word problems in math class occasionally kept me off that plaque at school. Yes, she was one of the classroom, band, and school leaders, and yes, she was always ready to help other students with their homework or music passages or with counseling a few friends to "do the right thing." As I remember those past years, I realize that the great values that twelve-year-old girl displayed … dedication, integrity, service, and determination to do what is right, regardless of the cost to herself… have not changed.

After high school graduation Dr. Lahr-Well and I took slightly different paths. I won a full, teaching scholarship and earned my B.S. degree from Illinois State University, where I majored in vocal music education, with minor degrees in English and history. I, then, attended Southern Illinois University at Edwardsville and earned my Master of Music degree. Dr. Almeda was awarded a full, teaching scholarship upon high school graduation and attended Southern Illinois University at Edwardsville for her B.A. degree, University of Illinois for her Master's Degree in Spanish and Italian languages and literatures (where she began her 50 years of teaching and administration in higher education), and St. Louis University for her Ph.D. in Spanish and Italian.

We reconnected in the mid-1980s, when she taught Spanish classes at our hometown community high school for a year and I was teaching vocal music and English for thirty of my thirty-four years in public education. Since we shared a lunch period, we had twenty-three minutes each school day to talk about many subjects, including the good and bad aspects of education, the crazy antics of the 'kids," and the endless paperwork. We both wanted the best opportunities and experiences for our students and were often in the counselors', principal's, and assistant principals' offices discussing students' problems and ways to correct them. Neither she nor I accepted a response like, "The student's 'fallen through the cracks' and there's nothing we can do about it!" or "It's too late to place that student in a special program now." As she taught her 30 - 35 students and I taught my 35 – 153 students per class, we made certain we covered the materials and tried to encourage and help each student – the average "kids," those very smart and talented students, and the slower or "lost" ones.

Putting a grade on a report card is easy; assessing each student's strengths and weaknesses and addressing those individual needs are difficult. Not every teacher or school district can or will discuss them, especially those needs of the extremely bright or marginally challenged "kids." It's bad enough to see your students hurt or denied opportunities because of administrative bureaucracy, but it was heartbreaking for Dr. Almeda to see her own children hurt when denied the educational opportunities through their school district that were rightfully theirs. If she couldn't help her own children, she would do everything in her power to see that neither this nor any other educational injustice was perpetrated against any other innocent child.

She had the experience, the knowledge, and the credentials to tackle such problems. Dr. Almeda M. Lahr-Well would "bite the bullet" and start her own school and build her own curriculum … a school and program that was then and is still superior to any other that I have seen.

As a public-school teacher of thirty-four years, I know the strengths and weaknesses of public-school education. While it is a good vehicle for large numbers of children, it is no longer an exceptional one. Sadly, I believe that if parents want the best education possible for their children, they must send them to the best private school with the best curriculum … the Lahr-Well Curriculum Concept. Each time I visit the Lahr-Well Academy I see students who are happy and actively engaged in their work … work that is far beyond what is being taught in the "traditional" education classrooms. These children use reasoning skills and vocabulary that is beyond that used in other schools by students of comparable ages. Tomorrow's leaders are being trained at this Academy, and parents, clergy, business leaders, private, and public school administrators need to take note.

I believe that this book will show readers what truly separates a mediocre to good education from this great one. Read with an open mind. All children deserve it.

Gail E. Mueller, M. Ed.

PREFACE

Education is "in my blood"! My parents spent over 70 years, combined, as teachers/administrators in a well-respected, public school system. They both had advanced-education degrees. They were both impressive examples of hard-working, success-focused mentors. I graduated from that public school system, and fulfilled my parents' expectation that I pursue university studies.

I completed my doctorate at a very young age. I was "ABD" (all but dissertation) when my husband Ralph and I married. My parents made me sign a contract with them that I would finish my degree by the end of the following year, or I would have to repay them for the wedding costs. I made the deadline, and continued on in the teaching field ... in almost every aspect of my life.

In my 50 years' experience as a university/college instructor/professor, I have noticed "a world of difference" in entering college freshmen. At first, I was able to "jump right in" with teaching Spanish and Italian; however, as the years progressed, I had to begin teaching English grammar, vocabulary, verb conjugations, moods, and parts of a sentence before I could even begin to teach the foreign languages.

I began noticing that many of these higher education freshmen could not write complete sentences in English, let alone write an entire paragraph. Fifteen years into my higher education professional experiences, I opened my own pre-kindergarten through grade 12 academy ... where I could educate (among other students) my husband's and my own children (and decades later ... grandchildren) ... hoping to better prepare them for "the university experience."

In the 35 years of Lahr-Well Academy, I have noticed the great discrepancy between the Academy's "accomplished" students and those in the general world around me. For all the high school **drop-outs**, for all the students **struggling**, for all the students **"left-behind"** ... (from academically-at-risk to learning-disabled to average to gifted), for all the students **lost**, for all the students who **"fell through the cracks,"** for all the students **whom the system has failed** to meet its obligation ... my heart goes out to you, and **this book** is for **your children and grandchildren**. Please pay close attention to what is happening in their academic lives. Test scores are necessary instruments to "take a child's **academic** pulse." However, it is important to know that these are simply **indicators** ... and not always accurate. Frequency of standardized tests (where the actual tests are **not** taught) are extremely helpful in establishing "ball park" grade equivalencies.

Parents, be mindful of "grade-inflation." If the test scores and potentially "inflated" grades are not compatible, **"something is rotten in"** SOMEWHERE! You need to give as close attention to your child's academic success as you do his/her sports accomplishments.

To all the dedicated teachers who over the centuries in the U.S. have passionately given your energy, your talents, your time, your money ... to buy classroom supplies ... I **applaud** you. To the system that controlled, constrained and conspired against you and the lost generations of students, I offer these observations.

INTRODUCTION

When the Twin Towers were decimated, **September 11, 2001**, American flags were proudly displayed throughout the country, and U.S. men and women were ready to fight and die for our precious "American Way of Life" ... **one** people with a **single**, **macro** culture ... **enhanced** by micro traditions! But **what has happened** to us in these past twenty years? Why have we abandoned our high American standards that had defined us as the leader of the free world? Why aren't we fighting to preserve for our children the rights and freedoms, ethics and values, and exceptional educational standards our enemies are **still** trying to rip from us? We, ourselves, are watching slip from the grasp of our children and grandchildren, those very rights, freedoms, ethics, values, and exceptional educational standards and achievements!

The American public has been **"sold a bill of goods,"** and now parents, religious leaders, business, industry, and the U.S. military need to **demand an immediate, proven remedy** to these U.S. education crises! Generations of students--millions of students--have been academically and morally lost! **Educational triage** is required **now**!

There are those among us who are revealing to the American people the dangers of **what has happened ... and what is happening** ... in U.S. education and government. For those of you who are doing so ... for the education critics mentioned (and not mentioned) here ... I believe you **care**! I **salute you ... and your efforts**! I believe you would be encouraged to know that **all is not lost!** Hundreds of books and articles have been written, exposing these problems ... especially in the K-12 public (traditional) sector, but a proven solution has not been offered ... until **now!**

This book addresses **what happened** to U.S. education (kindergarten through grade 12), and **what can happen to "fix it"!** It is about **reclaiming American Educational Exceptionalism**. It is about reclaiming our American heritage. It is about reclaiming our American values, ethics and morals. It is about **disruptive** education. It is about tailored education. It is about **SYNERGISTIC ACADEMICS** (patented and copyrighted). ... It is about the **Lahr-Well Curriculum Concept of Synergistic Academics** ... as implemented at **Lahr-Well Academy**, Edwardsville, Illinois, which has 35 years of proven, nationally-standardized test results' success!

In business, **synergy** is the concept that the combined value and performance of two companies will be greater than the sum of the separate individual parts. The term is often used with mergers and acquisitions. With **the Lahr-Well Curriculum Concept of Synergistic Academics**, synergy is the concept of the combined value and performance of all academic subjects ... and **how** those subjects relate to (interconnect with) ... each other!

Built on this curriculum of synergistic academics, America's next generations of business entrepreneurs, and critical thinking, problem-solving, **patriotic Americans** (students) are being trained with **the Lahr-Well Curriculum Concept** to become the local, national, and global leaders of the 21st century.

Reflecting upon **synergy** as the creation of a whole that is greater than the simple sum of its parts, let us take, for example, steel beams, wood, brick, mortar, glass, nails, screws, nuts and bolts. Lay these out on the ground, side by side, and you have nothing more than building materials. However, given a vision, a feasibility study, a design, financing, and a construction crew ... a skyscraper, a space center, or a **magnificent** cathedral can be the result of the synergy of these parts.

Similarly, why is it that education "experts" do not seem to understand that "building" a **magnificent** adult requires forging together mind, body, and spirit of elementary and secondary students through **synergistic academics ... weaving together (every year)** the threads of world history, American history, art, music, biology, chemistry, earth science, physics, algebra, geometry, composition (and more) ... with values, ethics, integrity and "good ole" American patriotism?

The pieces ... laid out side by side ... are simply that! ... Pieces! However, put together, the academic parts for a wholistic, complete ... synergistic curriculum, **and** the teaching-team to implement that curriculum, produces students of astonishing intellect and valor.

Parents, educators themselves, and clergy have been deceived for decades. Parents have been told that their children were (and still are) receiving an exceptional American education. They have been told that "exceptional" American education is still preparing their children with knowledge and abilities to enter the adult business, industry, science and technology worlds with **solid, basic** knowledge and exceptional educational skills. However, one needs only to check the student-global math and science ranking of the U.S. against other countries of the world to see how far the U.S. has fallen below even "third world" countries. If that weren't bad enough, just check U.S. illiteracy statistics and the percentage of high school dropouts.

Due to students' basic skills deficiencies and restrictive curriculum, educators soon learned, in too many cases, that they were unable to teach reasoning, logic, or critical (or creative) thinking. They were charged with the task of teaching (preparing for) the standardized tests, instead of teaching many of the course materials that could enhance the students' knowledge and/or appreciation of the materials. Then, for how many decades did we see dedicated, underpaid teachers striking for better pay ... along with newer books and fewer students in a classroom ... only to see those teachers return to the classroom with a few more dollars--but **outdated books** (if any) and **more** students to a classroom?

Ask a teacher about the *No Child Left Behind* program and what it accomplished in the classrooms. Admirable in intention ... **to leave no child (student) behind** ... the educator, **was supposed** to bring the lowest students "up" to higher (highest) levels. However, what happened ... more often than not ... resulted in the teacher, inadvertently, bringing the rest of the class "down" to the level of the lowest student. Not only were millions of the "lower" children left behind, millions of average and gifted students were (and are) left behind! **Yet, to hold any student back is to sabotage not only that student's future but also the global future of the United States!**

Clergy believed institutions of learning were reinforcing ethical behavior, honor and integrity. They, as well as American society, in general, believed that American history textbooks still taught about our American heroes and heroines. Little did they know that long-ago established, "conventional" American history books … where these American heroes and heroines had been presented … had been replaced by history books that would now portray many of **these heroes and heroines … and the U.S. itself … all as evil victimizers!**

In relaying this information and these statistics to you, the reader, … regarding the U.S. educational crises, and the answer I offer, I have chosen to quote from other authors (sometimes long passages) … not because I lack the ability to paraphrase. Rather, I believe the messages of these authors … to be exceptionally powerful messages … in their own words, and I do not want readers to think that I may have subjectively or mistakenly interpreted their words!

My general comments are in blue. Other authors' comments are in black. **The Lahr-Well Curriculum Concept of Synergistic Academics** (and other **Lahr-Well Academy** comments) are in red. Historical dates and program names are in black. Program and congressional acts dates are highlighted in yellow to emphasize to the reader the frequency and rapidity of replacement with which new trends, fashions, fads and dogmas have occurred (and still are occurring) in U.S. education … and the resulting, frequent failures of those programs … as well as to bring attention to--only a few of--the articles and books that have been written addressing the U.S. education crises resulting from this chaos! Green will suggest to business, industry, and the U.S. military that there is a way to **actually prepare** their future employees and/or military recruits **before high school graduation,** where graduates would already be working and testing well-beyond grade level, and where remedial courses in basic reading, math and English skills would never have to be taught!

I am hopeful that the colors will make it easier for you, the reader, to quickly distinguish whom it is that is speaking in the book.

Additionally, as a grammarian, I acknowledge that I frequently use "and" or "but" at the beginning of sentences. I know that grammar can be challenged! Also, I place most idioms in quotes. I choose their impact over more "sophisticated" vocabulary.

CHAPTER I

Why Phonics?

For over 400 years ... whether in establishing the thirteen colonies or in today's United States ... people from all over the world abandon their family, friends, and homelands looking for a better way of life ... the **American Way of Life**. But what does that **American Way of Life** entail? Our forefathers and mothers seem to have had a better understanding of that concept than we have today.

In 1908, Israel Zangwill introduces the term "melting pot" as a metaphor describing "Americanization" ... or the cultural assimilation of immigrants through their nationalities, their cultures, their ethnicities, **and the English language** ... as a **unified American Way of Life**. With the proud profession of the United States as this "melting pot," U.S. Americans are able to move, together, **unified** ... through the 18th, 19th, and first half of the 20th centuries with a vigorous fervor for God, family and country.

The Lahr-Well Curriculum Concept of Synergistic Academics builds on this foundation of God, family, and country through long-ago established "conventional" values and morality, intellect, skill mastery, national unity, the "American Way of Life," the "American Dream," as well as patriotism ... all on a daily basis ... to **all** students K4 (kindergarten students entering at age 4) through grade 12.

One of the first and foremost unifying factors in "Americanization" was, **and is**, the English language ... **the language of the United States of America**. (My doctorate is in Spanish and Italian linguistics. I greatly value these ... and other ... languages ... as well as the people and the cultures of those languages! **But ...** English** is the official language of the United States of America.) **And, one of the most powerful tools to teach English** was (**and is**) phonics! Today, however, in general, we as a nation are not teaching phonics. We are not even effectively teaching **English** to **every U.S. kindergarten through grade 12 student.**

The Lahr-Well Curriculum Concept of Synergistic Academics, however, utilizes **both seven years** of **phonics** instruction for teaching students to read (and for "sharpening" and reinforcing those skills), as well as a **whole language** (*see and say/sight word*) approach that utilizes 90 books ... based on phonetic levels of achievement. **The L-WCC/SA** approach prepares **all** K4 through grade twelve students with exceptional, English reading skills.

Yet, English alone does not solve the issue of cultural assimilation. Today, we don't **have** a **unified American Way of Life** ... English or not! Today we are a divided nation ... **no longer unified** in our language, culture, goals or values. Many of those immigrating to the United States **do not want** to

Americanize, but rather want to force the culture, goals and values of their original country onto those Americans of "the melting pot." We are now becoming a more splintered nation; and our educational system is, tragically, a prime example of how far away we have moved from our original tenets and the unity those tenets embraced. **American Exceptionalism** has become a "thing of the past."

Traditional U.S. education no longer provides for our children the **exceptional** standards of American education that, for more than four centuries encouraged high, fundamental standards, thought-provoking insights, pride in our nation, and the knowledge of our hard-fought rights and freedoms … that our enemies have repeatedly tried to destroy. As an educator of students from pre-kindergarten through college, for the past 50 years, I **know** what **has and has not worked … what is not** working!

Sadly, far too many of our U.S. educational textbooks have been "dumbed down" in reading, mathematics, natural sciences, geography, and world history. Parents, educators and clergy have been deceived, and have been unable to countermand these not-so-subtle attacks on U.S. education … **until now!** The question now is … what can be done about these great injustices to **our youth … the future America**?

As one might imagine, this did not all happen overnight … nor did it happen in "the blink of an eye." These deteriorations have been in process for almost 100 years! So, let's take a few steps back to see **what happened** … and **what can be "done to fix it"**!

In **1570,** Briton John **Hart** first introduced **the basic principles of phonics** to English-speaking children who were taught to read through the ABC method. With this method students recited the letters used in each word. The words generally came from a familiar piece of text. This was different from the spelling and reading methods used to teach European children. European children were taught the Romance languages (French, Italian, Portuguese, Romanian, and Spanish) … originating from Latin where there is almost a one-to-one sound to letter pattern correspondence. This meant that students could write/spell basically what they heard. That method didn't (and doesn't) work for English where, for instance, the single spelling "ough" produces, **at least**, **six** (some will say seven) **phonemes for the one "ough" grapheme:**

- though (like o in go)

- through (like oo in too)

- cough (like off in offer)

- rough (like uff in suffer)

- plough (like ow in flower)

- ought (like ȯ in saw)

It generally takes years of phonics and spelling practice to master this one vowel/consonant combination. Students, you say, can look in the dictionary for these spellings. Well, yes, eventually, they can learn to spell check; however, they must first learn how to spell! And with English spelling there is much more complexity … partly because it attempts to capture the 40+ phonemes of the spoken language with an alphabet composed of only 26 letters.

ALMEDA M. LAHR-WELL, Ph.D.

In the 16th century (in England), phonics becomes **the** method for teaching reading and writing of the English language … later becoming one of the foremost, unifying factors in Americanization. Phonics required (and still requires) a **solid** acquaintance with **phonemes** (alphabetical sounds). Then, in order for students to connect alphabetical sounds with the English spelling patterns that represent them (**graphemes**), students had to (and still have to) be able to hear, identify, modify, or move the phonemes. The objective of phonics was (and is) to help beginning English-speaking students (native or immigrant) to "decode" new, written words by sounding them out or by blending the sound-spelling patterns. In fact, trying to teach reading without teaching phonics would be similar to trying to teach spelling without teaching the alphabet … or trying to teach addition/subtraction/multiplication/division without teaching students how to count! Phonics proved to be an extremely effective method of teaching reading in the U.S. … from colonial times … until the late 1800s when government teamed up with educators to do "major surgery" (on what could have been "minor adjustments") … which eventually destroyed the solid, phonetic, reading foundation.

CHAPTER II

What Happened? ... 400 Years of U.S. Education History

In **1635**, the first Latin Grammar School (**Boston Latin School**) is established. This school, and others following it, are configured for the sons of certain social classes who are destined for leadership positions in the church, the state, or the courts.

In colonial times, reading instruction, based on phonics, is simple and effective. *The Bible* and some **patriotic writings** are among the first textbooks until *The New England Primer*, published in the late **1680s**. These resources not only build a foundation of intellect but of traditional values as well.

For more than 150 years, the educational foundation of reading is fortified. Students are learning to read well! **Then** in **1836, the McGuffey Readers** appear. These books are thought to better engage students. However, in the **middle of the 19ᵗʰ century**, a return to phoneme identification ... and how to decode words ... in order to be able to better spell, surface as a reading program of **synthetic phonics** (also known as **blended phonics** or **inductive phonics**). This method of teaching English-reading first teaches the **letter sounds ... phonics ...** and then the blending of these sounds together to achieve full pronunciation of whole words. **Synthetic phonics** is considered by some to be a more accelerated form of **phonics ...** leading to **"analytic" phonics**, where children were (and still are) taught to recognize words by sight (whole language/see and say), and later to break down the word into **smaller units of sound ... phonemes**. Perhaps the shift from giving students what they needed in a reading tool ... to what might engage them more ... was already demonstrating that, in order for students to become better readers and spellers of English, students needed a tool specifically designed for that purpose. Adding engaging reading material was supposed to be "icing on the cake."

From the **1890s to about 1910**, publishing companies begin focusing on books that will use simple language to retell classical stories and literature. **Then**, in the **early years of the 20ᵗʰ century**, critics complain that American schools are **too** academic, and are not preparing students for the "real" world. These complaints bring forth the first, significant, federal-education legislations: the Smith-Lever Act of **1914** and the Smith-Hughes Act of **1917**. These Acts encourage vocational education.

In the second quarter of the 20th century, Meaning-Based Curriculum begins to dominate, and by the 1930s and 1940s, reading programs become more comprehension-based with sight words in *Dick and Jane 1930*. Phonics no longer is to be an integral part of the reading curriculum. Spelling, as a subject, also continues to waver in and out of foundational curricula for the next century.

In the 1930s, the criticism is that schools are not meeting the needs of the youth or of the U.S. economy, and the 1933 Civilian Conservation Corps, a voluntary, public work-relief program is offered to unemployed, unmarried young men (originally ages 18-25 and later 17-28). This **program ceases operation in 1942.** The same 30s decade also brings to the U.S. the 1935 National Youth Administration program, a New Deal agency sponsored under the presidency of Franklin D. Roosevelt, to provide work and education for Americans between the ages of 16 and 25. This **program ceases in 1943.**

After World War II, when much of U.S. "traditional" education abandons phonics for a "whole language" approach (sight words/high frequency words/words in context, "See and Say"), reading test scores begin … **and continue today** … to fall!

Such is **not** the case with **the Lahr-Well Curriculum Concept** where **7 years** of **phonics** is taught to students, **as well as** a **whole language** approach that utilizes **90 books.** This whole language book series is actually based on a phonetic approach that introduces reading through vowels and vowel combinations: **short vowels**, **long vowels**, the **schwa** sound (an **unaccented** vowel/s … that generally makes the "uh" sound: ba.na´.na: … pronounced quickly, the 1st and 3rd syllables sound: **uh** in English), **dipthongs** (dif´-thongs: two vowels combined into one syllable the sound begins as one vowel and moves toward the other: *coin* and *loud*), **vowel** (and consonant) **digraphs** (a combination of two letters representing one sound: *ea* in feat or *ph* in phone), or **vowel-consonant-E** (c**ake**), and **silent E** (in other locations within words), etc.

At the end of WWII, in the latter years of the 1940s, when our soldiers return home, critics grumble that schools are underfunded and overcrowded. Additional criticism is that **now** the U.S. schools are **lacking in academic rigor.** Critics take the position that U.S. students are not prepared for the postwar economy, let alone the atomic age. So, just as U.S. education seems to be poised for an "excellence-overhaul," a significant educational "discovery" is made … a discovery that brings to attention the fact that the "once-primed" American educational system has not been moving toward excellence, but rather has been moving **from wavering to free-falling**!

And generations of U.S. students are lost!

Students lose reading, math, and English skills and abilities in the academic decline of educational skills as the government begins to gain control of the U.S. educational program. This results in texts that begin to "dumb-down" U.S. students. Many students lose the desire to even learn because neither they … nor their parents … any longer see the value of a high school education.

And more generations of U.S. students are lost!

In the 1950s, criticism begins to hit with more intensity, and so it is that in 1955, Rudolf Flesch's *Why Johnny Can't Read* [1] appears. In his book, Flesch criticizes the U.S. decision to drop phonics from its curriculum.

Flesch brings attention to the demise of American education! He explains that the only reasonable way to teach English is to teach the relationships between letters and sounds, and then teach how to combine those sounds into words.

Flesch calls the relationship between letters and sounds, and how they are combined into words, "intensive phonics" and explains that this is the European and Great Britain method of teaching English … because English is more difficult to teach (and to learn) than the standard European Romance and/or Germanic languages. He adds that European students tended to be reading, at least, one year earlier than anyone else. With this method, European children were about two years ahead of American children in academics. According to Flesch, children who are taught to read (only) by memorizing whole words by shape (as opposed to phonics) often tend to "end up" dyslexic or functionally illiterate.

Exceeding the standards of **"traditional"** education, **the Lahr-Well Curriculum Concept** teaches **7 years of phonics** … kindergarten through 6th grade, as well as reading comprehension through grade 12 … emphasizing, on a daily basis … spelling, vocabulary, composition, and **formal public-speaking.** Students begin to read at the age of 4, and somewhere during the age of 5, students read 90 books employing the phonics and spelling methods that fortify accomplished reading skills.

In 1957, the Soviets launch Sputnik, and traditional educators are blamed for losing the space race and jeopardizing the nation's security. Congress responds to this by passing the **National Defense Education Act (NDEA) of 1958.** This provides funding to all levels of U.S. education institutions in order to increase the technological power of the U.S. Additionally, **President Eisenhower** signs into existence the **Defense Advanced Research Projects Agency (DARPA)** of the U.S. Department of Defense, as well as the **National Aeronautics and Space Administration (NASA)** … both still in operation today.

Yet more generations of U.S. students are lost!

At this point in our country's history, educational "relevance" takes a lead position. Thomas Sowell, (Ph.D., African-American economist and social theorist, a senior fellow at the Hoover Institution at Stanford University, and the recipient of the Francis Boyer Award, the National Humanities Medal and the Bradley Prize) in *Inside American Education: The Decline, The Deception, The Dogmas,* reflects:

> Everyone wants education to be relevant. It is hard even to conceive why anyone would wish it to be irrelevant. Those who proclaim the need for "relevance" in education are fighting a straw man--and evading the crucial need to define what *they* mean by "relevance," and why that particular definition should prevail.

Beginning in the 1960s, insistence on "relevance" became widespread and the particular kind of "relevance" being sought was typically a relevance judged *in* advance by students who had not yet learned the particular things being judged, much less applied them in practice in the real world. Relevance thus became a label for the general belief that the usefulness or meaningfulness of information or training could be determined *a priori*.[2]

In one of his footnotes Sowell references a similar sentiment he finds in *Freedom to Learn for the 80's* by Carl Rogers. According to Sowell, Rogers believes that no one should have to learn something for which no relevance is seen. Rogers emphasizes that a student should be asked what he or she would want to learn; what things might puzzle the student; what the student is curious about; what issues concern the student; or what problems the student would like to solve.

However, how many elementary students are **curious about** or **find relevant** the multiplication tables or spelling? Or how many middle school students are **curious about** or **find relevant** natural sciences? Or how many high school students are **curious about** or **find relevant** composition and/or research papers? Yet society and U.S. technology, business and industry worlds demand that students, ideally, be proficient in these … and other … subjects … which may **not** seem relevant to the actual students!

Really? How can students … elementary, secondary, or, albeit, university or college freshmen or sophomores **"have a clue"** about what **will be relevant** to them in a field they either may have or may not have yet chosen? **Why** do we think high schools, colleges, and/or universities need academic counselors? **Students generally do not have *a priori* knowledge, and, therefore, do not have the information or experience required to be able to decide what they will find "relevant"** … especially when they do not "have a clue" about where they might be blessed to be employed! Once a "major" is declared, there is "a bit more" flexibility, yet, **the department** still "has the final say" about what **is and is not** "relevant."

Sowell observes:

> It is easy to see how this particular concept of relevance is consonant with trends toward more student choice, whether individually in choosing among elective courses in schools and colleges, or collectively in designing or helping to design the curriculum. Because the student has neither foreknowledge of the material to be learned nor experience in its application in the real world beyond the walls of the school, his emotional response to the material must be his guide.[3]

Sowell continues:

> It is hard to imagine how a small child, first learning the alphabet, can appreciate the full implications of learning these particular 26 abstract symbols in an arbitrarily fixed order. Yet this lifelong access to the intellectual treasures of centuries depends on his mastery of these symbols. His ability to organize and retrieve innumerable kinds of information, from sources ranging from encyclopedias to computers, depends on his memorizing that purely

arbitrary order. There is not the slightest reason in the world why a small child should be expected to grasp the significance of all this. Instead, he learns these symbols and this order because his parents and teachers want him to learn it--not because he sees its "relevance."[4]

Yet again, the educational "train" is derailed, and in the 1960s we find the open-classroom movement, which fades away in the 1970s; however, a light does momentarily shine, and the foreign language teachers of the United States offer a strong critique that the United States is far behind other world powers in teaching a second and/or third foreign language. With the establishment of the American Council on the Teaching of Foreign Languages (ACTFL) in (1967) foreign language instructors begin "making a case" for more intentional foreign language instruction in U.S. schools … (through the Foreign Language Elementary Experience: FLEX … and the Foreign Language in the Elementary School: FLES) beginning at the elementary level … when students "absorb" at a much faster pace because they have not yet formed the "mental blocks" that later appear in learning … such as: "But we **don't do it that way** in English!"

However, the foreign language foothold gained in the few decades following, soon begins to disappear; and current research, according to a **2017** report by the National Commission on Language Learning in the United States (a response to a Congressional request), states that only 58 percent of U.S. middle schools and 25 percent of U.S. elementary schools offered **… even one** foreign language in 2008.

And more generations of U.S. students are lost!

The Lahr-Well Curriculum Concept requires **5 foreign languages** (as well as English) from **all** students … beginning at age **4** … through age **18**! And while it is not the goal of **L-WCC/SA** to bring students to bilingual proficiency, it **is** the goal to give students varied and foundational abilities in learning foreign languages … in order to give them the skills and interests in embracing familiar … or unfamiliar … languages in the future.

Once again, "traditional" education abandons foreign languages and returns to a focus on reading; however, U.S. reading scores continue to fall. And in the 1970s whole language learning … learning vocabulary through context, and de-emphasizing phonics … is re-introduced as a **"new"** reading approach. Yet, research continues to show that early reading acquisition greatly depended … and **still** depends … on learning and understanding the connection between sounds and letters (phonics).

And more generations of U.S. students are lost!

In the 1970s, author and scholar **Charles Silberman,** American journalist and author, writes *Crisis in the Classroom: The Remaking of American* Education (1970) … commissioned by the Carnegie Corporation of New York. **Silberman** presents a strong critique of what he considers to be the many flaws in American education, most specifically in "mindlessness" and "routinization" of U.S. education, implying that students taught with these methods would "refuse or fail" to think! I believe this eventually leads to the 21st century academic declarations that **"memorization and regurgitation"** of facts have no value!

ALMEDA M. LAHR-WELL, Ph.D.

And more generations of U.S. students are lost!

The Lahr-Well Curriculum Concept of Synergistic Academics relies heavily on memorization of facts: (the English alphabet … addition, subtraction, multiplication, division **facts** … algebraic **formulas …** English grammar, punctuation, and composition **facts** … foreign language conversational phrases!), **while also** helping students (from 4 through 18) **build** on these **facts** … to critically think through connections of world history to American history to art to math to science to … etc., etc., etc., … **If** students do not know their "facts," how can they begin to formulate credible theories in critical thinking … to **solve problems**?

CHAPTER III

A Nation at Risk

In the 1980s, President Ronald Reagan "puts in place" a National Commission on Excellence in Education. The Commission's report takes the form of ***A Nation at Risk: The Imperative For Educational Reform* (April 1983).** The publication of this report is thought to be a "landmark event" in American educational history. It roused a reaction of the position that we had been, in effect, "committing an act of unthinking, unilateral educational disarmament."

Our Nation is at risk. Our once unchallenged preeminence in commerce, industry, science, and technological innovation is being overtaken by competitors throughout the world. This report is concerned with only one of the many causes and dimensions of the problem, but it is the one that undergirds American prosperity, security, and civility. We report to the American people that while we can take justifiable pride in what our schools and colleges have historically accomplished and contributed to the United States and the well-being of its people, the educational foundations of our society are presently being eroded by a rising tide of mediocrity that threatens our very future as a Nation and a people. What was unimaginable a generation ago has begun to occur--others are matching and surpassing our educational attainments.

If an unfriendly foreign power had attempted to impose on America the mediocre educational performance that exists today, we might well have viewed it as an act of war. (This author's emphasis) As it stands, **we** have allowed this to happen to ourselves. We have even squandered the gains in student achievement made in the wake of the Sputnik challenge. Moreover, we have dismantled essential support systems which helped make those gains possible. We have, in effect, been committing an act of unthinking, unilateral educational disarmament.[5]

The educational dimensions of the risk before us are amply documented in testimony received by the Commission. The report professes the following, numerous risk indicators (listed in black). **Words in bold** are this author's emphasis. **The Lahr-Well Curriculum Concept of Synergistic Academics** responses to the *Nation at Risk* indicators are in red.

• International comparisons of student achievement, completed a decade ago, reveal that on 19 academic tests American students were **never first or second** and, in comparison with other industrialized nations, were last seven times.	• After only 2-4 years' instruction with **Lahr-Well Curriculum Concept**, students test "at grade level" or 2-4 years above grade level. • (Exceptions are rare.)
• Some 23 million American adults are **functionally illiterate** by the simplest tests of everyday reading, writing, and comprehension.	• **All students** instructed with the **L-WCC**, receive **daily** instruction in reading, writing and comprehension … resulting in abilities at or above grade level.
• About 13 percent of all 17-year-olds [sic] in the United States can be considered functionally illiterate. **Functional illiteracy among minority youth** may run as high as 40 percent.	• Students entering kindergarten studies, as early as the age of 4, are generally reading by the end of the **first semester** … when instructed with the **L-WCC.** Students have high literacy scores due to receiving intensive, daily instruction in reading, writing and comprehension … as well as **many** other subjects. Minority youth also have exceptionally high literacy scores.
• Average achievement of high school students on most standardized tests is **now lower than 26 years ago** when Sputnik was launched. (Sputnik was launched in 1957.)	• Achievement on the IOWA Basic and ACT exams, for students instructed with the **L-WCC**, is **generally higher, and often substantially higher,** than national "norms."
• Over half the population of gifted students **do** [sic] **not match** their tested ability with comparable achievement in school.	• **All** students (academically-at-risk, learning-disabled, average, gifted) when instructed with the **L-WCC** are **helped to excel in their strengths** and **helped to eliminate their deficiencies**.
• The College Board's Scholastic Aptitude Tests (SAT) demonstrate a **virtually unbroken decline from 1963 to 1980.** Average verbal scores fell over 50 points and average mathematics scores dropped nearly 40 points. *	• **L-WCC** students, as young as 9 years of age have annually taken residual ACT exams since 1986. • **L-WCC** junior and senior scores are vastly superior to the national norm.

* Notice that even though the *Indicators Report* is from 1983, the Tawnell D. Hobbs' September 24, 2019 Wall Street Journal article: SAT Scores Fall as More Students Take the Test declares that scores continue to fall.

• (Overall, the combined mean **SAT score** is down to 1059, from 1068, out of a possible 1600 point scale for the two sections on the exam—math and reading, writing and language. The percentage of students meeting benchmarks to indicate readiness for introductory college-level coursework slipped to 45% from 47%. Sep 24, 2019)	• **All** high school students take the ACT annually at Lahr-Well Academy. Not **all** junior/senior students at Lahr-Well Academy take the SAT because the Midwest has generally required the ACT; however, those who have taken the SAT … as well as the ACT, have consistently shown **strong, "above-average" exam scores.** (**Is it any wonder why numerous colleges and universities are eliminating SAT/ ACT admissions requirements?**)
Return to *Indicators Report*: • College Board achievement tests also reveal consistent declines in recent years in such subjects as physics and English. • **Not** meeting **any** of the benchmarks increased to 30% from 27%.	• With the **L-WCC**, English grammar and English composition are required, annual subjects for **all students.** • It is the listed intention in the Curriculum Concept that **all** juniors and/or seniors be advanced enough to study physics at the Academy. We continue to work in that direction.
• Both the number and proportion of students demonstrating superior achievement on the SATs (i.e., those with scores of 650 or higher) have also dramatically declined.	• While **students** of the **L-WCC have proven themselves over and over again with the ACT,** we have only begun to annually encourage juniors and seniors to take the SAT.
• Many 17-year-olds [sic] **do not possess the "higher order" intellectual skills** we should expect of them. Nearly 40 percent cannot draw inferences from written material; only one-fifth can write a persuasive essay; and only one-third can solve a mathematics problem requiring several steps.	• The **L-WCC**, is designed to instruct **all** students in "higher order" intellectual skills; in daily critical thinking skills; in general composition … including persuasive essays; and in daily solving of mathematical word problems … requiring several steps.

ALMEDA M. LAHR-WELL, Ph.D.

• There was a **steady decline in science achievement scores** of U.S. 17-year-olds [sic] as measured by national assessments of science in 1969, 1973, and 1977.	• With the **L-WCC t**here is a continual and **steady incline in science achievement scores of all** students. • **All** students (except for 4 or 5 years-old) take daily science vocabulary tests in biology, chemistry, earth science, and/or physics … from the time a student is 6 (and reading well) through the age of 18. • **All** students receive daily activities and/or experiments in biology, chemistry, earth science, or physics … from age 4 through AP Biology or Chemistry.
• Between 1975 and 1980, **remedial mathematics courses in public 4-year colleges** increased by 72 percent and now constitute one-quarter of all mathematics courses taught in those institutions. More recent statistics show a higher percentage in remedial courses.	• There is **no need for remedial mathematics (or remedial English)** courses in public 4-year colleges with the **L-WCC** students … due to extensive training and advanced scores in both subjects.
• **Business and military leaders complain** that they are required to spend millions of dollars on costly remedial education and training programs in such basic skills as reading, writing, spelling, and computation.	• Students graduating from **Lahr-Well Academy have no need** for **any kind** of remedial work in reading, writing, spelling or computation. By the time students graduate, at 16, 17, or 18, students are testing far beyond grade-level.
• **The Department of the Navy**, for example, reported to the Commission that **one-quarter of its recent recruits cannot read at the ninth grade level**, the minimum needed simply to understand written safety instructions. Without remedial work they cannot even begin, much less complete, the sophisticated training essential in much of the modern military.	• **It might be wise** for the military to establish **preparatory schools (leasing the Lahr-Well Curriculum Concept)** for their own bases. Not only would students receive **exceptional** academic, civic and patriotic instruction, as well as character-development instruction, but they could also begin to receive early military training … giving those students earned advantages and **incentives for entry into the armed services.**

The *Indicators of the Risk* report adds: "These deficiencies come at a time when the demand for highly skilled workers in new fields is accelerating rapidly."

• Computers and computer-controlled equipment are penetrating every aspect of our lives: homes, factories, and offices.	• From the age of 4 through high school graduation, **L-WCC** students receive daily instruction, on a quarterly basis, in Keyboarding, Google Suite, Coding and Introductory Cyber Security ... on a quarterly basis.
• One estimate indicates that by the turn of the century millions of jobs will involve **laser technology and robotics**.	• From the age of 4 through high school graduation, **L-WCC** students receive **weekly instruction in either: robotics, electronics, avionics, engineering, and/ or elementary direct and alternating current fundamentals.**
• **Technology** is radically transforming a host of other occupations. They include health care, medical science, energy production, food processing, construction, and building repair, and maintenance of sophisticated scientific, educational, military, and industrial equipment.	• Business, industry and armed services could establish preparatory schools (**leasing the Lahr-Well Curriculum Concept**) for the children of their employees. Not only would the students be extremely well-prepared in academics, they would also have extensive training in values, ethics, morals, as well as character-development instruction, in addition to civic and patriotic training. • By creating a **Lahr-Well Curriculum Concept program,** with students beginning as young as ages 4, 5, or 6, students could complete their high school academics one to two years early, graduate early, and begin internships with the company ... at an early age. The businesses could require a one to two-year internship as repayment for elementary and secondary education.

Unfortunately, for most U.S. students, **the** U.S. "traditional," educational world **moves on toward unimaginable decline and self-destruction,** oblivious to what has happened (and to what is happening).

And more generations of U.S. students are lost!

Fortunately, for **the Lahr-Well Curriculum Concept of Synergistic Academics** students ... **the Concept** has already **proven itself,** over decades, **to reverse** *The Nation at Risk's* **declared unimaginable decline.** The other end of the spectrum has been (and is) offered ... where students achieve **unimaginable educational excellence.**

ALMEDA M. LAHR-WELL, Ph.D.

CHAPTER IV

Determined to Self-Destruct

In **1990,** the largest and oldest voucher program begins in Milwaukee, Wisconsin. (Vouchers provide students, generally from low-income families, a government-funded scholarship to attend a participating, private school.) Today vouchers exist in 15 states and the District of Columbia; and while there have been both anecdotal successes and failures, vouchers do not provide a standard base of educational elements. Additionally, very few U.S. students are given the voucher opportunity.

In **2007,** Utah passes legislation that creates the first statewide, universal voucher program … available to **any** student in the state … with no eligibility limitations. A successful petition effort places the legislation on the state ballot for voter approval, but in November **2007,** the legislation is voted down (except for the already-existing, special needs voucher program). The new voucher program is never implemented.

And more generations of U.S. students are lost!

In **2011,** Indiana creates the nation's first statewide school voucher program for low-income students. **But more generations of U.S. students … from other income levels … are lost!**

Outcome-Based Education, or Outcomes-Based Education (OBE) takes root in the U.S. in **1994.** This educational **theory** is structured around projected **outcomes** where, at the completion of the educational experience, the student should have achieved the stated goals. Once again, there was neither a single, specified teaching style nor a standardized assessment in OBE, but simply acquiring knowledge did not (and does not) allow for a measurement of the ability to use and apply the knowledge in different ways. This method also seems to have "come and gone" without having a significant impact upon U.S. education or its students.

So once again a new trend is adopted throughout the land … with no means … and no plans for … measuring any kind of outcome … sounding much like the MGM Mickey Rooney and Judy Garland musical where Mickey shouts, "Hey, let's put on a show!" In this case, the OBE shouts, "Hey, let's put on **another** show!" **(Trends and fashions and fads … Oh, my!)**

And more generations of U.S. students are lost!

On the heels of **OBE** comes the **charter movement**. From 1991 to March, 2015, 43 states and the District of Columbia enact charter school laws. In 1994 Congress authorizes the **Public Charter School Program** through **Title X** (ten) of the **Elementary and Secondary Education Act.** However, many states blocked (and continue to block) charter school programs through state laws and lawsuits.

And more generations of U.S. students are lost!

Book after book, article after article fill U.S. shelves with concerns about the U.S. education system and the millions of children being lost in it! **Many** of those are written already before 1993.

Faith Keenan, "8ᵗʰ-Grade Students No Math Whizzes," *San Francisco Examiner,* June 6, 1991.

Paul Hollander, *Anti-Americanism: Critiques at Home and Abroad, 1965-1990* (New York: Oxford University Press, 1992).

Curtis C. McKnight, et al., *The Underachieving Curriculum: Assessing U.S. School Mathematics from an International Perspective* (Chicago: Stripes Publishing Co., 1987).

Karen DeWitt, "Verbal Scores Hit New Low in Scholastic Aptitude Tests," *New York Times,* August 27, 1991.

Susan Dodge, "Poorer Preparation for College Found in 25-Year Study of Freshman," *The Chronicle of Higher Education*, November 20, 1991.

Bill Richards, "Wanting Workers," *The Wall Street Journal,* Supplement, February 9, 1990.

"The Myth Debunked—Spending Not the Cure-All for Schools," *Education Update* (Heritage Foundation), Fall 1990.

Chester E. Finn, Jr., *We Must Take Charge: Our Schools and Our Future* (New York: The Free Press, 1991).

Lewis J. Perlman, "The 'Acanemia' Deception," Hudson Institution Briefing Paper, No. 120, May 1990.

Thomas Toch, *In the Name of Excellence: The Struggle to Reform the Nation's School, Why It's Failing, and What Should Be Done* (New York: Oxford University Press, 1991).

Sue Berryman, *Who Will Do Science?* (New York: The Rockefeller Foundation, 1983).

Ten years after *The Nation at Risk Report,* when the U.S. should have been reaping the rewards of educational repair, Thomas Sowell writes *Inside American Education: The Decline, The Deception, The Dogmas* (1993). At the time, **Sowell** is a senior fellow at the renowned Hoover Institution where he specializes in social and economic policy and the history of ideas.

The inside cover of **Sowell's** book announces what should have warranted the attention of a three-alarm fire, but the U.S. educational system and the public move on as if someone had merely lit a candle!

Sowell offers,

> Virtually everyone has heard how poorly American students perform, whether compared to foreign students or to American students of a generation ago. What everyone may not know are the specifics of how bad the situation has become, how and why the public has been **deceived,** or the **dogmas** and **hidden agendas** behind it all.[6]

(This author's emphasis)

HOW DID THIS HAPPEN IN THE LAND OF THE FREE AND THE HOME OF THE BRAVE?

The critic who assesses Sowell's **book says,**

> Our educational establishment—a vast tax-supported empire existing quasi-independently within American society—is morally and intellectually bankrupt, charges distinguished economist and social critic Thomas Sowell. And in this top-to-bottom tour of the mismanaged institutions, cynical leadership, and tendentious programs of American education, Sowell exposes the numerous 'deceptions and dogmas' that have concealed or sought to justify the steep and very dangerous decline in our educational standards and practices across the board.

> Among the more serious ills of American education are the technically sophisticated brainwashing techniques now being applied to children and teenagers in so-called 'affective education' programs; the special 'peace' and 'nuclear' education programs that actively promote 'politically correct' attitudes; **the 'values clarification' and sex education curricula that portray parental and religious authority figures as agents of repressive and unjust social and political orthodoxy**; and the racial 'mini-establishments' created on college campuses by minority demagogues and complaisant administrators that enshrine a self-serving ideological double standard, thus betraying the real interests of minority students.

> Sowell's exhaustively researched investigation draws particular attention to the wide array of textbooks and other instructional materials, promoted with astonishing success by a multi-million dollar industry styling itself a 'secular humanist' movement, which fosters these ideas—ideas that are **not just anti-American, Sowell maintains, but essentially totalitarian in character.** These sinister curricular developments, combined with often cowardly and irresponsible management more concerned about institutional image and ranking than with fiscal integrity or a commitment to educate our youth, will breed disaster unless immediate steps are taken to reform the entire educational system.[7]

(This author's emphasis)

Sowell predicts the impending demise of U.S. education almost 30 years before ... long before ... the turn of the 21st century. Disaster, indeed, has overcome U.S. education, much like the 1958 American science-fiction horror film *The Blob* ... with the storyline of an alien amoeboidal entity that, coming to Earth from outer space ... inside a meteorite ... crashes and grows larger, redder, and increasingly more aggressive as it devours citizens in a small community.

As **Sowell** suggests, our educational establishment **is,** indeed, a "vast tax-supported empire" existing almost independently within the U.S. ... especially if one were to take into consideration that our "traditional," **tax-supported education monopoly** is the **only** "business" entity in the U.S., other than the federal government itself, that is **protected from free enterprise** ... with the exception of a few successful parochial and private schools, and the more recent charter schools. In some states, the local, "traditional" school district receives the tax dollars of students attending parochial and private schools within the district! **So, while the "traditional" system receives the tax dollars/per student ... the parochial and private schools receive the expense of educating those students!** Just imagine what would happen if parochial and private schools would close their doors in those districts ... especially where districts are already facing financial bankruptcy! The "traditional" system would have to absorb the extra expense of educating those additional hundreds, if not thousands, of students.

And more generations of students are ... and would be ... lost!

ALMEDA M. LAHR-WELL, Ph.D.

CHAPTER V

The Answer to the Tax-Supported Empire ... Monopoly

As a tax-supported empire, U.S. "traditional" education has been able to continue its downward spiral, dumbing down and indoctrinating generations of U.S. students, while **being guaranteed protection from** free enterprise, **and** ... at the same time, **basking in billions** of U.S. tax-payer dollars.

Sowell states that for a very long time, he finds the low quality and continuing deterioration of American education, within the tax-supported empire, to be appalling. As he builds the foundation of his criticism, he sweeps through the U.S. "State of Education" with a profusion of charges in multiple areas of the "American Way of Life" that translate into the derogation of American education. Among those observations is the U.S. education's vast tax-supported empire.

Already back in 1983, Sowell exposes that huge teachers unions (NEA and AFT) have "large sums of money available to support political lobbying, and significant blocs of votes to throw onto the scales at election time."[8] With hundreds of employees and well over $100 million dollars a year, Sowell explains that the NEA, in particular, has "vast sums of money available for political purposes and for propaganda campaigns to get the public to see the world as the (union) sees it ... to equate bigger school budgets with better education."[9] Sowell goes on to profess that while there seems to be an educational sense of entitlement to other people's money, the sense of needing to justify teachers' (or students') performance seems to be lacking. (This author's inserts)

As Sowell references alternatives to "traditional" education, he mentions the uphill battle school choice faces against the educational establishment and their media allies. He lists the following as the most common objections given:

1. Parents would make bad choices.

2. Parents who make good choices would take their children out of substandard schools, leaving behind in hopelessness the children of parents with less knowledge, concern, or initiative. (The nerve!!! ... This author's reaction)

3. Parental choice would destroy the American tradition of the common school for all, replacing it with schools segregated by race, income, religion, and other social divisions.

4. It would lead to an unconstitutional government subsidy of religious schools.

5. It would be prohibitively expensive.[10]

1.&2. The assumption here is that parents lack the knowledge, interest, and initiative to make choices that would be as good as the choices made by the education establishment.

3. Common knowledge has proven that many parochial, private, (and now charter) schools have strong interracial, inter-income, inter-religions, and other inter social divisions that provide schools with student-ratio "balance."

4. The question of "unconstitutional government subsidy of religious schools" is for the U.S. courts to decide.

5. The "expense" often proves to be much less than that of "traditional" schools. (The **2018 Illinois Policy Report**—based on the 2015 U.S. Census Bureau Annual Survey of School System Finances, supports this statement. **Direct quotes from the Report are in black.**) The Report headlines read: **Illinois Spends More on Education, But Outcomes Lag: Misplaced priorities in Illinois' education system may be the reason students are less prepared for college than peers in other states.**

The 2015 U.S. Census/Illinois Policy Report supports what Sowell has already noted in 1993. According to the Policy Report, Illinoisans spent **$13,797 per student on K-12 public education in fiscal year (2015)** … This represents spending that is **the highest in the region and 13th highest in the nation.** Sixty-three percent of these dollars, in 2015, come from local, **extraordinarily high, property tax burdens.** However, Illinoisans aren't seeing a good ROI (Return on Investment). **In fact, public schools, through some of the most highly funded in the nation, fail to prepare their students for college.** In 2015 those students test below the national average in ACT composite scores.

Illinois spending on education per student among highest in the Midwest

Per-pupil K-12 education spending adjusted for cost of living, fiscal year 2015

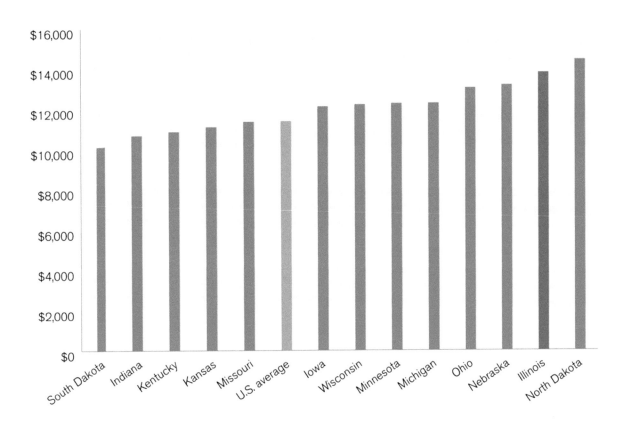

Source: U.S. Census Bureau Annual Survey of School System Finances, adjusted using Bureau of Economic Analysis (Regional Price Parity table)

@illinoispolicy

Despite Illinois spending more than most states on education, Illinois is decidedly in the middle of the pack when it comes to test scores, and below the national average in ACT composite scores.

Illinois students trail nation in college readiness
ACT scores for graduating class of 2015, Illinois vs. U.S. average

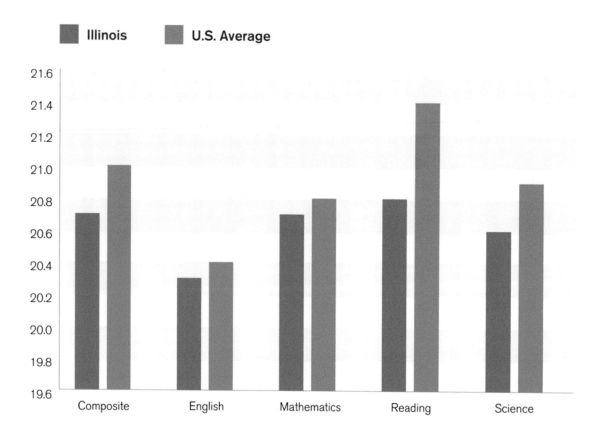

Source: U.S. Census Bureau Annual Survey of School System Finances, adjusted using Bureau of Economic Analysis (Regional Price Parity table)

@illinoispolicy

Where are the tax dollars going?

Although Illinoisans have been repeatedly told that the only way to get better results for students is to pour more money into the system, this is not the case. Other states spend less but get better results.

Illinois is ranked 8th in the nation in administrative spending as a percentage of education spending, according to U.S. Census Bureau data. In other words, a good chunk of Illinoisans' property tax dollars don't make it to their child's classroom. Instead, those dollars went to fund bloated administration costs that stem from having more than 850 school districts.

ALMEDA M. LAHR-WELL, Ph.D.

Other states do more with less

The fact that other states do more with less illustrates more education spending isn't a necessary condition for better outcomes. A number of states that spend less money per student than Illinois are seeing better results in national test scores.

Take a look at Virginia, for example.

Virginia local governments are only slightly less dependent on property tax collections, which make up 35 percent of their revenues, while Illinois property tax collections make up 40 percent of local government revenues.

However, Virginians have a property tax burden that is 24 percent lower, and an overall tax burden that is 29 percent lower than what Illinoisans face.

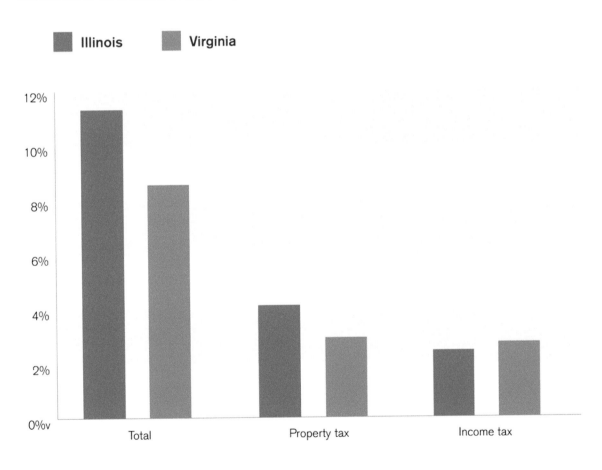

Virginians enjoy lower total tax burden, lower property tax burden than Illinoisans
Tax burdens as a share of income, 2015

Source: U.S. Census Bureau Annual Survey of School System Finances, adjusted using Bureau of Economic Analysis (Regional Price Parity table)

@illinoispolicy

Meanwhile, Virginia's public school system has a higher four-year high school graduation rate and better prepares its students for college than Illinois'. ACT scores in Illinois (the dominant standardized college admission test in the state) were 1.4 percent below the national average, while SAT scores in Virginia (the dominant test in that state) were 2.9 percent above the national average.

Virginia students are better prepared for college than Illinois students
Average test scores of graduating high-school class compared to national average, graduating class of 2015

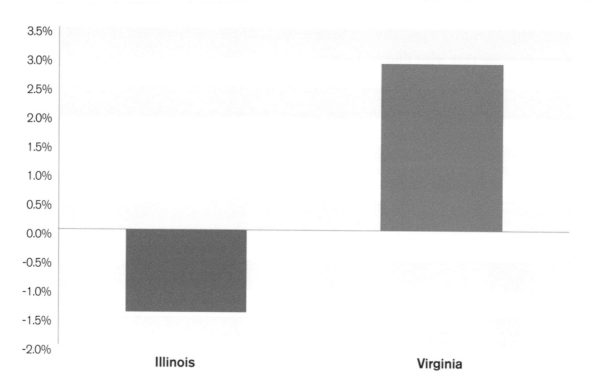

Note: Illinois figure uses ACT scores vs. national average and Virginia figure uses SAT scores vs. national average, as those are the predominant tests in each state.

Source: Virginia Department of Education, Illinois State Board of Education

@illinoispolicy

How does Virginia accomplish this?

Virginia manages to ensure better educational outcomes for its students than Illinois despite spending 20.5 percent less per student. How? Virginia accomplishes this because it has created an education system that makes student and instructional spending the top priority.

(Illinoispolicy.org/Illinois-spends-more-on-education-but-outcomes-lag/: Bryce Hill, Senior Analyst; Joe Tabor Senior Policy Analyst/Education February 25, 2015)

ALMEDA M. LAHR-WELL, Ph.D.

Just 4 years later another Illinois Policy Report, based on the 2019 U.S. Census, brandishes the following declaration: "Bureaucrats Over Classrooms: Illinois Wastes Millions of Education Dollars on Unnecessary Layers of Administration." The report notes that Illinoisans face the second-highest property tax rates in the nation. Tax-dollars spent per student are among the highest in the Midwest, but student outcomes lag.

The obvious question that arises from these statistics is "**Why?**" The answer suggests in the report is that too many of those education dollars become trapped in bureaucracy before reaching the classroom. The report expands on that response, offering that in the past 4 years, Illinois public schools employ fewer teachers and have fewer students. However, the number of administrators grows.

The 2019 report "drives home" the point by comparing the $15,337.00 per-student spending to Grade 8 proficiencies. The proficiencies are 36% in reading and 32% in math. **Would this be the ROI** (Return on Investment) **you would hope for with dollars you would personally invest?**

Such is not the case with Lahr-Well Academy. The per-student expenditure is **less than 40%** of the 2019 Illinoisan per-student expenditure … and the reading and math proficiencies **exceed grades above** chronological ages.

In juxtaposition to the vast tax-supported empire is the **Lahr-Well Academy,** a **not-for-profit business** that **does not receive any** federal or state tax dollars as an educational institution! The **one** tax advantage the Academy appreciatively receives is not to pay a purchase tax on supplies. Other than that, the Academy incurs the expense of the normal payroll and unemployment taxes as does any commercial U.S. business. So, the Academy is not tax-supported. It receives **no** annual, financial support from the federal or state governments. (However, this summer … 2020 … with Coronavirus Pandemic, **as a small-business**, the Academy **did** benefit from the PPP.)

Unlike the U.S. "protected" tax-supported monopoly, **Lahr-Well Academy** has remained financially independent … without the aid of tax-dollars. It has fought through 35 years of "system" challenges to emerge as a **maverick** in the U.S. education system … as an **educational disrupter** … inspiring students to embrace life-long learning and strong, moral integrity.

CHAPTER VI

U.S. "Traditional" Education's Moral and Intellectual Bankruptcy

If you will recall, **ten years after** *The Nation at Risk Report,* Sowell writes *Inside American Education: The Decline, The Deception, The Dogmas* where he makes the following observations:

> Much has been said about how our young people do not meet the academic standards of their peers in other countries with which we compete economically. While this is both true and important, their academic deficiencies are only half the story. All across this country, the school curriculum has been invaded by psychological-conditioning programs which not only take up time sorely needed for intellectual development, but also promote an emotionalized and *anti-intellectual* way of responding to the challenges facing every individual and every society. Worst of all, the psychotherapeutic curriculum systematically undermines the parent-child relationship and the shared values which make a society possible.

> I am frankly surprised that the results are not even worse than they are ... The incredibly counterproductive fads, fashions, and dogmas of American education—from kindergarten to the colleges—have yet to take their full toll, in part because all the standards of earlier times have not yet been completely eroded away. But the inevitable retirement of an older generation of teachers and professors must leave the new trends (and their accompanying Newspeak) as the dominant influence on the shaping of education in the generations to come.[11]

Rest assured, **the Lahr-Well Curriculum Concept** does not implement counterproductive fads, fashions, and dogmas of "traditional" American education. From kindergarten to high school graduation, **the L-WCC** is built around the concept of the "Renaissance" man/woman, as well as problem-solving, creative thinking, critical-thinking skills and other knowledge needed for democratic decision-making.

For many decades, the U.S. education system takes the position that fads, fashions, and dogmas would produce more-competent students. And, of course, the fads, fashions, and dogmas always require more tax-payer dollars. However, numerous studies, over these same decades show that while the U.S. ranks **near** the top in over-all per-pupil expenditure, the performance of its students often ranks at or near the bottom ... all while new anti-intellectualism, anti-patriotism, anti-parental respect gain a stronger and stronger foothold!

Sowell's response to this is: "Too many American students learn neither an intellectual process nor a knowledge base, nor acquire habits of study."[12] In fact, Sowell takes the position that "the process of making public school textbooks easier to read has been going on so long and so widely that it has even acquired a well-known generic name ... "dumbing down.""[13]

The Lahr-Well Curriculum Concept of Synergistic Academics vehemently rejects "dumbing down." **The Curriculum** is built upon an intellectual process, a knowledge base, habits of study, patriotism, and respect for the parent-child-educator relationships ... emphasizing moral values which add to an enhanced society of responsible, independent individuals who work together for the common good of all.

While all of the **Sowell** anti-isms grow, he notes the continuing decline in academic performance, yet a continuing rise in GPAs. He quotes from Cooperative Institutional Research Program, *The American Freshman: National Norms for Fall 1989* and *1990:*

> Significantly, this era (now **these eras**) of declining academic performance has also been a period of rising grades. American high schools gave out approximately twice as many C's as A's in 1966, but by 1978 the A's actually exceeded the C's.[14] By 1990, more than one-fifth of all entering freshmen in college averaged A minus or above for their entire high school careers. At private universities, entering freshmen with averages of A minus or above were an absolute majority—54 percent.[15]

There is **neither declining academic performance nor grade inflation** with the **L-WCC!** Students are expected to "master" the skills as those skills appear in the **Progression of Curriculum** within **the Concept:**

Progression	4/5 yrs old	5/6 yrs old	7-11 yrs old	12-18 yrs old	Field Trips	
English	x	x	x	x		archaeological
Chinese	x	x	x	x	Cahokia Mounds	dig
French	x	x	x	x	StL Science Center	
German	x	x	x	x	StL Art Museum	
Italian	x	x	x	x	StL Zoo	
Spanish	x	x	x	x	StL Botanical Gardens	
Lord's Prayer:E,C,F,G,I,S	also Armor of God in English				StL History Museum	

Subject					Place	Notes
Chess	x	x	x	x	StL Genome Institute	
					StL Ren/Bar Churches	Roman/ Gothic
Math	x	x	x	x	StL Basilicas	
Math Word Problems	x	x	x	x	Greek/Russian Ortho	
Phonics	x	x	(Kthrough6th)		Jewish Synagogue	
Reading	x	x	x	x	Relleke Pumpkin Farm	
Reading Comp	x	x	x	x	Fitz's Root Beer	
World Geography	x	x	x	x	Scott Joplin House	to be added
Penmanship	x	x	x	x	Old StL Capitol Bldg	Dred Scott Reenactment
STEaM:					Springfield Museum	Lincoln
Hands-on Art	x	x	x	x	StL Holocaust Museum	
Music Appreciation	x	x	x	x	Fed. Reserve Bank of St. L	
Veggie Tales	x				Piasa Bird	
Biology		x	x	x	Alton Underground Railroad	
Chemistry		x	x	x	Alton Lock & Dam	
Earth Science		x	x	x	Lewis and Clark Museum	
Physics		x	x	x	Mother Jones Museum	Mt. Olive, IL
Engineering		x	x	x	Greenville Dairy Farm	
Robotics		x	x	x	Edwardsville Fire House	
Measurement		x	x	x	Lake Williamson Camp	
Place Values		x	x	x		

ALMEDA M. LAHR-WELL, PH.D.

					Animated Bible Stories	
Fractions		x	x	x	Animated Bible Stories	
Decimals			x	x	Animated Classics	
Percents & Equivalents			x	x	Legends & Folk Tales	
Time		x	x	x		
Money		x	x	x	Patriotism	
Map Skills		x	x	x	Service Projects	
Charts		x	x	x		
Graphs		x	x	x	**Advance by ability**	**not by age**
Squares to 25			x	x		
Roman Numerals			x	x	Family Environment	
English Grammar		x	x	x	Caring Environment	
Composition		x	x	x		
Critical Thinking		x	x	x		
Macro/Micro Econ.			x	x	Extra-Curricular Suggestions	
World History	x	x	x	x	Select Sports	
U.S. History	x	x	x	x	Recreational Sports	
U.S. Constitution			x	x	Suzuki	
Illinois Constitution			x	x	Alton Youth Sympho	
Compu Skills: Typing		x	x	x	StL Youth Symphony	
Computer Programming		x	x	x	Girl Scouts	
Algebra I			x	x	Boy Scouts	
Geometry			x	x	etc.	
Algebra II/Trig				x		
Pre-Calculus				x		
Calculus				x		
World Lit Master			x	x		
World Philosophy			x	x		
Public Speaking	x	x	x	x		

The **L-WCC** introduces all these subjects at multiple grade levels and challenges students to achieve … **generally-above** "traditionally-designated" grade competencies. So, while **Lahr-Well Academy** students are presented this amazingly-challenging and encompassing curriculum, they are mastering the information at levels **generally years-above** their chronological ages! During these academic studies, **L-WCC** students are also preparing to become local, national, and global leaders … all the while learning about U.S. patriotism.

Returning to Sowell's concern with rising grades (in "traditional" education), we find that he additionally draws attention to declining test scores. He emphasizes that those two trends are, by no means, unconnected.

> Without this systematic deception of parents and the public by rising grades, it is highly unlikely that the decline in performance could have continued so long. The deeper question is—**Why? Whose purposes are being served, and whose agendas are being advanced**, as American education declines?[16] (This author's emphasis)

The systematic deception of parents and the public is found in numerous areas of "traditional" education. It also includes the "traditional" system discouraging parents from sending their children to a parochial, private, or charter school, or to homeschool their children. The system tells parents that they do not want to choose any program that is "not accredited," should they want their child/ren to be accepted into colleges and universities. This is far from the truth. **Lahr-Well Academy,** while **state registered,** is **intentionally not-accredited …** to avoid state or federal control of its curriculum. Its students have never been denied entrance into colleges or universities, including an Ivy League school.

In fact, recent headlines help to further dispel the accreditation myth. On September 3, 2015, this headline appears in *Business Insider*: **There's a new path to Harvard and it's not in the classroom.**[17] The article presents the facts that homeschooling students are being accepted into Ivy League schools, and lists as an example 18-year-old Claire Dickson entering Harvard in the fall of 2015. **If** "traditional" U.S. accreditation were "the **defining** answer/the requirement," students educated in other ways would not be accepted into institutions of higher education.

If you recall, the **National Commission on Education Report (1983)** addresses the concern about the national decline in math and science scores. Ten years later, Sowell reaffirms the continuing decline in math and science, as well as other subject areas:

Sowell presses:

> When nearly one-third of American 17-year-olds [sic] do not know that Abraham Lincoln wrote the Emancipation Proclamation, when nearly half do not know who Josef Stalin was, and when about 30 percent could not locate Britain on a map of Europe,[17] then it is clear that American educational deficiencies extend far beyond mathematics.[18]

ALMEDA M. LAHR-WELL, Ph.D.

He continues:

> The Brutal Reality is that the American system of education is bankrupt. Allowed to continue as it is, it will absorb ever more vast resources, without any appreciable improvement in the quality of its output, which is already falling behind world standards.[19]

Sadly, one-fifth of the way into the 21st century, the appalling waste of financial resources, with the continuing decline in the quality of educational achievements have proven **Sowell** to be "dead-spot on"!

At the conclusion of his book *Inside American Education* Sowell offers:

> This is not a blanket condemnation of every aspect of American education. Even an enterprise in bankruptcy often has valuable assets. Both the assets and the liabilities of our educational system need to be assessed, to see what can be salvaged from the debacle and reorganized into a viable enterprise.[20]

However, anti-intellectualism ... anti-patriotism ... anti-parental respect ... dumbing-down curricula ... declining test scores ... inflated grades ... not knowing Lincoln from Stalin ... all lead back to Sowell's previous pressing questions ... Why? Whose purposes are being served? Whose agendas are being advanced?

Read on ... to the end of the book! ... You will find answers to all 3 of these questions!

Reeling from all of the anti-isms, it is no wonder that more and more U.S. students are demanding socialism and Marxism, when they have no idea what either of these actually means! However, the **L-WCC/ SA** teaches about anarchism, Christian Democracy, Communism, Fascism, Marxism, Libertarianism, Nationalism, Populism, Progressivism, Socialism, as well as a democratic republic, or democracy and republic, etc. It is critical that high school and college students better understand the government choices they have and/or demand!

Sir Winston Churchill offers his perception on some of these governments ... perceptions that need to be shared with students studying world governmental systems. Churchill professes: The inherent drawback of capitalism is the unequal distribution of wealth; the inherent dignity of socialism is the equal distribution of poverty. While this should "say it all" to students, **the L-WCC** encourages students to study more--to better understand the different types of government systems. The students can then use this knowledge, in addition to their critical and analytical skills, to assess the freedoms and liberties they stand to lose should an enemy, or "friend," or the students themselves, as U.S. citizens, be successful in destroying the democratic-republic of the United States ... either through ignorance, deception, or aggression! Being well-versed on the good and the evil of these government systems, and implementing the skills of critical thinking, help students dispel the fear of being uninformed-Americans who could be easily manipulated. Students are taught the Judeo-Christian values on which the U.S. Constitution is based, and how these religious morals have been ... and are ... **the values on which U.S. patriotism and ingenuity are built!** The teachers also emphasize that, while encouraging students to be business entrepreneurs and problem-solvers, they also caution students to guard against individual, group, and national greed--which has led to the downfall of great (and sometimes not-so-great) nations. Students are taught to **constructively** critique themselves, their environments, and their governments … throughout life!

L-WCC teachers emphasize that while students must respect teachers, and other "authoritarian" figures, students, as they reach "maturity," should never "blindly" accept what is taught, heard, or seen … as "gospel." Rather students must use the analytical and critical skills taught them to try to reach "enlightened" positions of their own. Provided these analytical and critical skills, **L-WCC** students are given the tools to discern the potential dangers of anarchism, Communism, Fascism, Marxism, Socialism etc.

The **L-WCC** teaches the value of long-ago established, "conventional" U.S. and world history. At the same time students are cautioned about the mistakes nations, groups of individuals, and individuals themselves make in seizing power over others ... where one group has rights denied to other groups. **The Curriculum** also teaches students that these concepts, while being monitored and adjusted … for the good of all … cannot be maligned to the extent of devaluing and attempting to erase one's own history. Teachers of **the L-WCC** encourage students that they **always** need to **constructively** critique themselves and their environments! They teach students that individuals, nations, and religions need to acknowledge evil where evil exists, yet learn from the good … in order to build healthy and respectful national societies that can operate in partnership with global societies.

And here … no generations of (L-WCC) **students are lost!**

Colleges and universities also embrace the decline of U.S. education and the deception that camouflages it. Unfortunately, now that ACT and SAT scores continue to drop, U.S. colleges and universities are beginning to eliminate those requirements. Is this another deception? This action deserves a much better answer than to be "passed off" as simply "equity." Sowell's comment on this is "Whether blatant or subtle, brainwashing has become a major, time-consuming activity in American Education at all levels."[21]

There is no deception nor are there dogmas taught with the **L-WCC/SA.** Parents are always allowed to know exactly what information is in the textbooks--the curriculum utilized. Even as **the Curriculum Concept** is integrated into **Lahr-Well Academy**, evolution and creationism are taught side by side--with the expressed statement to parents that both are taught as "theory." It is "up to" the parents to profess their own beliefs to their children. **The Academy** has had the privilege in the last 35 years of educating children of the Christian, Jewish, Buddhist, as well as Islamic faiths**. The Academy** allows students of other beliefs to be excused from required memorization of the Christian elements of the **Curriculum**. However, the **Curriculum Concept** teaches students about Buddhism, Christianity, Hinduism, Islam, and Judaism, in a manner as factual as possible … highlighting the virtues and vices of each as expressed through world history, art, architecture, music, literature and philosophy … while, at the same time, giving and teaching respect of other faiths … as long as the faiths of others do not teach repression or persecution of anyone of a different faith. However, the Academy **is** a Christian Academy, and students are well prepared as Christian **apologists** … not apologizing for their faith, but rather intellectually and spiritually **ready to defend** their Christian faith!

With **the L-WCC/SA**, by the time a student is reading at the 6th or 7th grade reading level, he or she is first placed into the AP American History text (AP=Advanced Placement … a label used for "college-preparatory" classes. For the **Academy**, we use the term to apply to college level textbooks … only). The **L-WCC** *American History* text still includes our "conventional" American heroes from which students study for their remaining years at the Academy. The following year an AP world history text is added; then a (college-level) condensed 272 pieces of world literature, **as well as**, a (college-level) text of 70 world philosophers (80 philosophical works). Once introduced, these texts are required every remaining year.

There will be those critics, educators as well as lay persons, who will say: 1) "That **has** to be '**boring**' for students to study from the same book each year." I say, "Students, as well as business entrepreneurs or biblical scholars, do **not** master massive amounts of information in just one year! Additionally, humans process information, or "see" information differently at different ages due to maturity and life experiences. Therefore, "seemingly boring" information is often viewed and/or processed as "new"!

Critics may also say, 2) "Those students are not reading the **complete work** of … Shakespeare." While students **do** study the complete works of several authors during their time at **the Academy**, once they have begun the *Masterpieces of World Literature*, students, **before they enter college,** know the time line, the story-line/plot, the major characters, **as well as** literary critiques of **272 world literary masterpieces …** from the "beginning of time" well into the 20th--and now the 21st centuries! With this, students already have an amazing advantage in what many professionals would consider "freshman lit" classes.

To add to this, while many of our U.S. colleges and universities no longer require philosophy for **all** students, at **Lahr-Well Academy**, **some** students as young as middle school **and all** high school students study 70 world philosophers and 80 of their philosophical works. Students, who have been instructed with the **Lahr-Well Curriculum Concept**, have amazingly advanced insights into numerous fields of philosophical areas, as well as significant, in-depth understanding of humanity, and of society.

The extent to which **the L-WCC** embraces "affective" **education programs** (helping students develop personal belief systems, emotions and attitudes), is **not** the generic, traditional **"It's all about me!"** educational component. Instead, the **L-WCC** attempts to help each student develop a **positive, constructive belief system**--first in him/herself, then within the family--and finally within society. Students are helped to develop a "balanced" emotional presence, and are helped to become self-assured … while at the same time becoming empathetic to others. Political correctness is **not** taught, but **the Golden Rule** of doing unto others as you would have them do unto you (as modeled and practiced by staff) **is** taught. **The L-WCC** "affective" education programs teach **"It's all about us … as community!"**

Secular humanism (the belief that humanity is capable of morality and self-fulfillment without belief in God) is **not** taught … **nor is** anti-Americanism … **nor is** a promotion of the U.S. moving to a totalitarian/socialistic/Marxist/communist government taught through **the Lahr-Well Curriculum Concept.** What **is** taught is an understanding of and respect for the U.S. democratic republic … to the extent that every student recites the Pledge of Allegiance daily (except those who are not U.S. citizens). Additionally, every student is taught yearly the Preamble to the Constitution, the 27 Amendments, as well as the *Gettysburg Address*. While students are taught to respect our country, they are also taught to be vigilant of what is happening at all levels of government. They are constantly encouraged to take personal responsibility in monitoring and protecting their U.S. freedoms. Students are taught that it is their moral duty to accept this personal responsibility ... supporting that **the L-WCC** is **not** morally bankrupt, but rather intrinsically rich in moral integrity.

Sowell references the morally and intellectually bankrupt U.S. "traditional" education system in his book *Inside American Education: The Decline, The Deception, The Dogmas.* This bankruptcy became apparent to me, a little earlier, in the late 70s during my years at McKendree College/now McKendree University, in Illinois. In 1979, about 15 years after the first U.S. English as a Second Language (ESL) program was established in Florida, I wrote and directed one of the earliest university ESL programs in the country. It was our program's objective to bring international students to campus, and to give them one semester of intense ESL (English as a Second Language) instruction, after which they would enroll in the college/university. These Latin American students, as young as 15 and 16, were being admitted into a United States college ... when our own U.S. students were not coming in until, generally ages 18 or 19. I eventually became intrigued by the age differences and began asking myself why, when the United States was recognized as a leading, scientifically and technologically advanced, super-power ... why our students were not prepared for colleges and universities at a much younger age?

Barring the educational politics of keeping U.S. students in high school longer "for the extra tax dollars," a second explanation that I was soon to discover was that many U.S. parents had begun (even a few decades earlier) to **pamper** their children ... to the extent of **actually stunting** their mental, social, emotional and academic growth. This was the beginning of what we would see develop in our country with so many "supposed-adults" graduating from college, yet returning to their parents' basements to live!

We were becoming a nation of hovering "helicopter" parents who relieved our college-aged "adults" of personal responsibility. Should the student not succeed, it immediately became the "fault" of the professors or the school, itself. Then, when we were not watching, anti-American history became the "staple" of, not only college/university American history, but elementary and secondary American history, as well! Little did we know that **our U.S. students were being indoctrinated instead of educated!**

However, as a nation, we were doing a **great** job with sports! Families were at practices and games **multiple** times during the week, **encouraging, coaching, and cheering** their elementary, secondary, and college/university students on to greater accomplishments!

Academics and intelligent achievement were "taking a back burner" in school ... and in life. It was no longer appealing nor exciting for one's child to speak and write in a scholarly fashion, nor to problem-solve, nor to master critical-thinking skills. International students and international professionals would now be "filling the bankrupt-void" of our U.S. intellectual "job" positions.

The **Lahr-Well Curriculum Concept of Synergistic Academics is an answer** to this bankruptcy! Its proven academic record **leaps** out, shouting, **"Here I am! Look at me!"** The L-WCC touts what many would consider "unimaginable" **academic and intellectual achievements ... accompanied by some "good ol'-fashioned" morals, respect, values and discipline!** The L-WCC adds to that foundation--self-respect, respect for others, dignity in one's work, and the **Golden Rule.**

ALMEDA M. LAHR-WELL, Ph.D.

During the past 35 years, with **the Lahr-Well Curriculum Concept**, nationally-standardized test scores prove that students, "across the board" (academically-at-risk, learning-disabled, average and gifted) from K4 through grade 12, have been achieving at an unimaginable pace, more often than not, 2-4 years above chronological age ... after 2-4 years' instruction in **the Curriculum**. Gifted students, after 4-6 years' instruction, more often, test 4-6 years above chronological age!

You say, "Impossible"? Here are the statistics to prove otherwise!

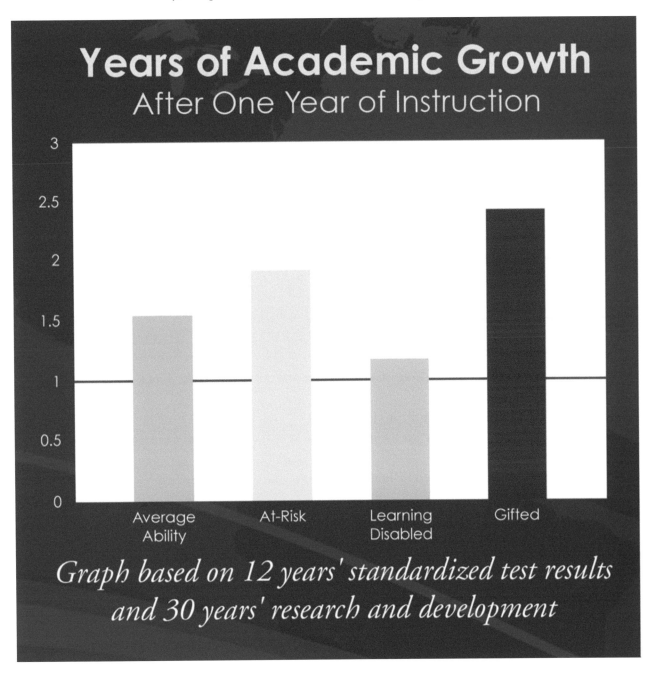

I say, **"Come visit Lahr-Well Academy and see how it works!"**

CHAPTER VII

Myth Buster: True or False? More Money=Better Education

FALSE! More money does not necessarily equal better education!

What has happened? Instead of more money = better education, we have seen, up to this point, more money poured into program after program, trend after fashion after fad after dogma … with the end results being not only **"Johnny can't read,"** in the 1950s, **but also** the crisis point in the U.S. "State of Literacy" … which eventually becomes a general U.S. "Crises in Education"!

The culmination of what has been happening for decades in U.S. Education is highlighted in *Crisis Point: The State of Literacy in America* (Resilient Educator: 2020 … direct quotes):

The United States is facing a literacy crisis. Yes, crisis. It isn't new, but its impacts upon our kids, our economy, and our society are far-reaching and expanding. How bad is it? Take a look at some numbers.

- More than 30 million adults in the United States cannot read, write, or do basic math above a third-grade level. — *ProLiteracy*

- Children whose parents have low literacy levels have a 72 percent chance of being at the lowest reading levels themselves. These children are more likely to get poor grades, display behavioral problems, have high absentee rates, repeat school years, or drop out. — *National Bureau of Economic Research (NBER)*

- 75 percent of state prison inmates did not complete high school or can be classified as low literate. — *Rand Report: Evaluating the Effectiveness of Correctional Education*

- Low literacy is said to be connected to over $230 billion a year in health care costs because almost half of Americans cannot read well enough to comprehend health information, incurring higher costs. — *American Journal of Public Health*

When one cannot read, one's self-esteem generally suffers! Sowell similarly observes "the self- esteem doctrine" as "just one in a long line of educational dogmas used to justify or camouflage a historic retreat from academic education."[22]

The **Lahr-Well Curriculum Concept** successfully implements self-esteem within the confines of academic challenges of disciplined and superior work, and the ability to present such work in a calm, self-assured manner of public speaking, as well as written competency.

Having addressed self-esteem, Sowell turns to double standards as the "essence of political correctness" and challenges "traditional" education's social agendas of his time … which continue into our time. In the **Lahr-Well Curriculum Concept,** political correctness is **not taught.** Social Agendas are **non-existent.**

Sowell moves, then, from self-esteem, through political correctness and social agendas to the dangers of education-athletics vs. education-academics both in "traditional" K4 through grade 12, as well as within the educational framework of colleges/universities. While the **Lahr-Well Curriculum Concept** acknowledges the importance of athletics, **Lahr-Well Academy** offers no sports; however, the curriculum **does** include one-half hour daily of physical exercise (in a gym), or training outside on our many community bike-trails for a 5K walk-training where **all** students are expected to participate. Additionally, parents are encouraged to find sports events and teams within the community-athletic arena, as well as the YMCA, Boy Scouts, Girl Scouts, churches or other community organizations. Within these programs students can experience larger group participation which reinforces interaction of students of different cultures, socio/economic classes, skills or abilities.

Decades after Sowell, the following article, authored by Amanda Ripley, is written for the October 2013 issue of *The Atlantic*, an American magazine. Its title: "The Case Against High-School Sports"

The United States routinely spends more tax dollars per high-school athlete than per high-school math student—unlike most countries worldwide. And we wonder why we lag in international education rankings?

> Sports are embedded in American schools in a way they are not almost anywhere else. Yet this difference hardly ever comes up in domestic debates about America's international mediocrity in education. **(The U.S. ranks 31st on the same international math test.)** The challenges we do talk about are real ones, from undertrained teachers to entrenched poverty. But what to make of this other glaring reality, and the signal it sends to children, parents, and teachers about the very purpose of school? (This author's emphasis)

And More, More, More Money continues to Dumb, Dumb, Dumb-Down Our Kids … More and More.

Another daunting book of the 1990s decade is titled: ***Dumbing Down Our Kids: Why American Children Feel Good About Themselves But Can't Read, Write, Or Add*** by Charles J. Sykes, Ph.D. (1995).

At the time of his authoring this book, Sykes, a senior fellow at the Wisconsin Policy Research Institute, a university and parent-group lecturer about the subject of schooling, had already authored three previous books, and was recognized as a journalist specializing in education issues. Sykes sends a very similar message to that of Sowell.

The book's critic offers:

> Our kids rank near to, or at the bottom of, international tests in math and science. National reading scores continue to fall. Despite increases in spending, our schools persist in turning out children lacking in basic skills and knowledge—children who are wholly unprepared to compete in the twenty-first century. While the educational establishment points its finger at society, families, and television, Charles Sykes focuses on the schools themselves.[23]

In his book, Sykes argues that the school wars of the 1990s would be the redefining cultural and political debate of our time, while many school systems and parents bask in the glow of complacency about their own children's education. *Dumbing Down Our Kids* documents the **collapse of standards** in our schools, **the flight from learning**, and **the triumph of mediocre, feel-good education** that was more concerned with pumping up self-esteem than it was with passing on knowledge.

> This **dubious triumph (of dumbing-down)** includes the latest (1994) educational fad, Outcome Based Education. Although known by different names in some states, OBE was the most recent in a long series of "reforms" that had eroded our schools. Charles Sykes traced these fads from their roots in the early "progressive" theories of John Dewey, through Dick and Jane and Spot, and into Life Adjustment, New Math, Mastery Learning, and other **reforms-gone-wrong**.[24]

(This author's emphasis and insert)

With examples drawn from schools around our nation, Sykes discussed:

- Why American students test poorly in language, math, and science when compared with peers from other countries.

- Why "self-esteem" has supplanted grades and genuine achievements in our schools.

- How the education establishment, teachers' unions, and school boards lower standards in our schools while continuing to raise budgets and taxes.

- How curriculum and standard tests are being dumbed down so everyone can pass but no one can excel.

- Political correctness from kindergarten through high school: how schools, not parents, teach moral "values."

- Why many good teachers burn out or are discouraged, while bad ones are rewarded.[25]

ALMEDA M. LAHR-WELL, Ph.D.

Although there are **numerous** pages that I could cite, let me just **respond** to the opening observations in Sykes' book, while at the same time encouraging my readers to "digest" both Sowell's and Sykes' books … as well as each of the other books I cite in **my** book.

Referencing Sykes' research, the **Lahr-Well Curriculum Concept of Synergistic Academics**, is **not** in crisis!

The following list of details explains the **(L-WCC) "no-crisis" status:**

- The **Concept's** Academic Calendar is based on a **year-round calendar** (with 2 weeks of morning instruction at the end of June and beginning of July) **or a 10-month calendar** … with 4 quarters (8/9 weeks) … followed by 2 to 3 weeks' break between each quarter.
(This accounts for some of the amazing academic gains.)

- Its students' **overall** scores are years above their chronological ages, after 2-4 years of instruction!

- **In all exams its students rank at the top** of their national, chronologically-aged classes in reading, English, math and science.

- The Concept persistently produces **students advanced in basic skills and knowledge** … preparing them to compete in the 21st century.

- Neither mediocrity nor complacency about basic skills and knowledge has ever been accepted.

- **Exceptionally high standards** are put into place **for each and every student.**

- There is an **immersion into learning** for **every** student.

- Knowledge and well-being are the primary intents of the **Concept**.

- **Self-esteem** is emphasized through **the Golden Rule** and **public speaking.**

- The latest educational trends, fashions and fads are nonexistent within the **Concept**.

- When compared to peers within the U.S. its **students test very high in language, math, and science.**

- **Genuine achievements** are still the major focus of the **Concept**.

- **The U.S. education establishment has no control over the high standards** offered through the **Concept.**

- The **Concept** (as implemented at **Lahr-Well Academy**) **does not accept** any state or federal funding. This limits the power of government to dictate curriculum.

- **Each year every student** (beginning at age 4 or 5 and continuing through grade 12) takes the *Iowa Test of Basic Skills* (ITBS), testing Language Arts, Reading, Math, Science and Social Sciences, and composition … thus eliminating the possibility of parents discovering (as many do within the "traditional" educational system) that **their child cannot read** at the end of 3rd grade … a time when most "traditional" schools **begin** standardized testing.

- **All** upper, middle-school-aged students, and all high school students take the ACT yearly … as the Academy researches the possibility of adding the SAT into the annual group of standardized tests.

- **All** students take an in-house, nationally-standardized exam 3 times yearly:

    first day of school

    end of first semester

    end of school year

These tests help the staff keep its "finger on the pulse" of each student. **No child "falls through the cracks"** at the **Academy. No child has ever been "left behind!"**

CHAPTER VIII

Twenty-First Century NCLB and Much More...

In the early 21st century, when **No Child Left Behind (NCLB)** becomes the new, governing law for K-12 U.S. education, as signed into law in **2000,** by President George W. Bush, this now is the most recent modification to the Elementary and Secondary Education Act of **1965.** This law is **supposed to hold schools accountable** for how students learn and achieve. By 2015, even with **some** growth in reading and math, the law is overridden by yet another, newer law!

The Lahr-Well Curriculum Concept never adopted No Child Left Behind; and, in its 35 years of existence, the **L-WCC** has **never left a child behind!**

In **2001,** on the heels of **No Child Left Behind,** rise not one, but two new programs: **U.S. STEM and STEaM:** Science, Technology, Engineering, (art), and Mathematics ... as introduced by scientific administrators at the U.S. National Science Foundation (NSF). (I have Art in parenthesis because, of course, it is left out of the original formula.) Yes, it is critical that our U.S. students know science, technology, engineering, mathematics, **and** art; but it is just as critical that our U.S. students know social science, patriotism, philosophy, foreign languages, and critical thinking! Of course, one could say, "Oh, it's **assumed** that these other subjects will be taught!" But as we are already seeing, these other subjects are being ignored ... if not, outright, "thrown out of" K-12 curriculum.

One of the greatest challenges of **STEM/STEaM** will be to offer advanced high school scientific concepts that can be built on elementary and middle school/junior high science foundations. The success at the high school level will somewhat depend on whether or not grade school and middle school natural sciences adequately prepare students for more intense-advanced studies at the high school level.

While **STEM/STEaM** are introduced only recently ... early in the 21st century, the **L-WCC** had implemented those very programs, on its own in 1985 along with all the other subjects listed in the **L-WCC Progression of Subjects**. Basic electronics, engineering, robotics, and avionics, as well as keyboarding, basic computer-programming, web-design, and an introduction to cyber-security have been added more recently to the **L-WCC**. And although the foundational subject areas have never changed, **the Lahr-Well Curriculum Concept is a living, breathing entity**, and is constantly reevaluated and enhanced as part of its continued R&D (Research and Development).

Another unique and exceptional element of the **L-WCC** is that it doesn't matter if a student is male, female, white, black, Latino, Asian, Christian, Jew or whomever. **Every** student **is pushed beyond** his/her "comfort zone" to become the best intellectual leader he or she can be! Neither does it matter that a student will lead in a household, on a citizen's local board, at the state, national, or international level, the student will be prepared to offer integrity, intellect, valor, yet empathy, in **all** that he/she does … to make this country … this world … a better place!

While there will be those naysayers who might be alarmed at "pushing students out of their comfort zone," it needs to be acknowledged that we grow only when we are "pushed out of" (or voluntarily step/leap out of) our comfort zones. Would an athletic coach say to a student, "Oh, don't practice throwing free shots for hours! That might put too much stress on you!" Or … **"Don't try to jump higher, run faster, or swim better!"** So, why do educational, medical and psychological "experts" and/or parents want to hold their children back from striving for greater academic gains? Of course, too much of anything can be bad, and "the team-teachers/leaders" need to constantly observe, evaluate, and adjust. When a student reaches an impasse, **then** is the time to take one or two steps back … and "run in place." **If** a student stops, or is stopped, before he/she reaches an impasse, neither the student (nor the teacher) will ever know how much the student **could have succeeded … or exceeded!**

In 2001, The Partnership for 21ˢᵗ Century Skills is initiated. It was (and is) to synchronize the age-old "3R's" of curriculum content with the new "4C's" needed for 21ˢᵗ-century learners: That is to say:

- Reading

- Writing and

- Rithmetic with

- Critical thinking and problem solving

- Communication

- Collaboration, and

- Creativity and innovation

Later, to these 7 skills is added:

- Information literacy (the study or use of computer and telecommunication systems for storing, retrieving, or sending information).

ALMEDA M. LAHR-WELL, Ph.D.

Yet later, to the seven and one 21ˢᵗ Century Skills, are added:

- Media literacy: hardware, software or tool that composes, creates, produces, delivers and manages media: audio, video, images, information, interactive (media), video games, virtual reality and augmented reality environments

- (Computer) Technology literacy: application of scientific knowledge for practical purposes, particularly in industry (engineering or applied sciences)

- Flexibility: (according to the Partnership for 21ˢᵗ Century Skills): willingness to make necessary compromises in order to accomplish a group's common goal … incorporating feedback, praise, setbacks, and criticism.

For me, the **flexibility component** creates an additional challenge here. I have seen information in early math skill instruction *(new math)* where the **"goal"** is to have students arrive at a **compromised** (intentional dual meaning: a **compromised process**, as well as a **compromised answer**) solution. In this type of exercise, it is more important to have students **compromise** (work together as a group) than it is to have the group arrive at the **correct** answer. **So**, when students gather together to work in a group to add **3 plus 2** … and **compromise** in order to arrive at **an answer of 4**, students are praised for working together to arrive at an agreed upon **"compromised"** answer! **But** what has happened to teaching the students **the correct answer … with or without compromise**?

As if these **compromised** methods, weren't bad enough, when one adds the "new math" method to the compromised method, is it any wonder why students are falling further and further behind in math skills?

Donna **Hearne** specifically addresses this in her *The Long War and Common Core* (2015), where she gives a specific example of what has happened (and is happening) in U.S. education.

She states,

> Across America moms and dads are struggling to help their children complete homework that frequently brings the student and sometimes the parents to tears. How would you help your grade school child solve this homework multiplication problem?

Multiply 164 times 72.

Common Core Math Uses:

```
PARTIAL PRODUCTS METHOD
 164    164    164    164    164    164    164    164
x  72  x  72  x  72  x  72  x  72  x  72  x  72  x  72
          8      8      8      8      8      8    1  8
               120    120    120    120    120    120
                      200    200    200    200    200
                             280    280    280    280
                                   4200   4200   4200
                                         7000  +7000
                                               11,808
```

OR

```
LATTICE METHOD
     1   6   4
 1  [0/4] [2/8]  7
 1  [0/2] [1/0] [8]  2
     8   0   8
```

Traditional Math Uses:

```
STANDARD ALGORITHM METHOD
      164
   x   72
      328
     1148
    11,808
```

The performance of the Lattice and Partial Products Methods do not make sense to you, because you remember being taught to use the Standard Algorithm Method.[26]

The actual "new math" instruction presents a convoluted approach to what used to be "simple" math!

And more generations of students are lost!

The Partnership for 21st Century Skills was designed to involve the entire school community … educators, students, families, businesses, community, and others … to create an enduring impact for every child.

Notice! Natural sciences, art, foreign languages, social sciences, literature and philosophy are **not even mentioned!** Yet The Partnership, supposedly, proposed to integrate the original seven skills with core academic subjects such as English, reading or language arts, world languages, art, mathematics, economics, and science.

So, from 2001 to 2020, as educational budgets continue to be cut, how many schools teach world languages now … and in which grades?

ALMEDA M. LAHR-WELL, Ph.D.

The **L-WCC** offers (and has offered for 35 years) **all 7 of the 21ˢᵗ Century Skills, including many more** … in addition to foreign (world) languages! The Concept **offers 5 foreign languages for every student K4 through grade 12!** We are adding a **6ᵗʰ language** in 2020-2021!

How many schools teach art now … and in which grades?

The **L-WCC** offers **weekly hands-on art** (through world history) K4 through grade 12, **and music history** (through world history) K4 through grade 12!

How many schools offer economics … and in which grades?

The **L-WCC** offers **macro and micro economics** to students K4 through grade 12!

How many schools offer biology, chemistry, earth science, physics, engineering, robotics, and avionics … and in which grades?

The **L-WCC** offers biology, chemistry, earth science, physics, engineering, robotics, and avionics Grade 1 through Grade 12.

So, how can The Partnership for 21ˢᵗ Century Skills integrate **all** these skills in **all** of these areas when several of the areas no longer are taught in "traditional" schools? This is **a troubling question** for U.S. education, in general, but **not for** the **Lahr-Well Curriculum Concept**! Now … with the coronavirus pandemic and social-distancing requirements, some U.S. school districts are considering cutting school attendance in half (3/2) as a schedule for students … 3 days one week, alternated with 2 days the following week. How will districts be able to effectively cover one year's material in only one-half year?

Some districts, will, in fact, be continuing "forced-in-home" learning where many students do not have access to the necessary electronics. Before this pandemic, students were already behind. With the 3 month "shut-down" in the spring semester, students fell even further and further behind. **Now** with potential extended-in-home schooling, or 3/2 weeks, **students will not only be left behind, they won't even be "invited on the trip"!**

Take into consideration that The Partnership for 21ˢᵗ Century Skills was (and is) to be **for every child …** and **almost twenty years after its creation, how many of your children** have been in this program, let alone experienced positive results from this program? Actually … how many of **you have even heard of** the program?

Just a few years after The Partnership for 21ˢᵗ Century Skills (2001), when educators were teaching students that it was more important to work together as a group (compromise) than it was to find the correct answer, John Stossel's *Stupid in America: Are our kids being cheated out of a good education?* airs in 2006. Stossel, an American consumer television personality and author, produces a piece that sets the U.S. educational system on edge. Stossel makes a statistical case, comparing test results of American students to those of Belgian students. His final analysis challenges the U.S. **education monopoly**. Yet, even beyond that, one of the You Tube comments (generated by Stossel's video), offered by Nick Trice, adds an additional, astute observation: **No amount of money will solve the problems caused by a culture of ignorance, anti-intellectualism, base materialism and poor parenting.**

With the results "fresh in our minds," we need to take a step back to recapture some of the many U.S. trends, fashions and fads in education. We have moved from **Progressive Education** of the 1930s, through **Mastery Learning, Moral Relevancy/No Absolutes, Outcome-Based Education, America 2000, Goals 2000**, *No Child Left Behind, Race to the Top,* **Differentiated Learning,** and … waiting in the wings … **Common Core!**

While all of these programs sound exciting and hopeful, U.S. reading and math scores continue to fall within national and international testing results. (Granted, one can take into consideration that some of those test scores might be challenged--to the extent that not **all** students in other countries, take similar tests; **however,** not **all** U.S. students take those tests either! But, specific U.S. test scores, compared state to state, profess similar results … **still declining reading and math scores!**

Yet in 2009, parents seem to surrender more educational control to their states, and without **really knowing** the intent or the content of the program, enthusiastically embrace *The Common Core State Standards Initiative,* a state-led effort of the National Governors Association. That is to say … it was enthusiastically embraced … at least … **initially!!!**

The initial **Common Core State Standards (CCSS)**, introduced in 2009, was (is) a concept that state education leaders and legislators pushed to identify what students would know in the areas of English / language arts and mathematics.

Author James R. Delisle, (Ph.D. teacher, professor and father), addresses **CCSS** in *Dumbing Down America: The War on Our Nation's Brightest Young Minds.* **Delisle** brings to the public's attention that as early as 2013, more than 40 states had adopted all or part of the **CCSS**. [27]

Delisle points out that one of the early questions arising from **CCSS** implementation was, "what happens when a child comes into a particular subject or grade level *already knowing* the core standards?"[28]

Although it is impossible to "guess exactly" what each student knows and doesn't know, the question of "already knowing" information is **not an issue** for the **Lahr-Well Curriculum Concept**. **Discerning** (as accurately as possible) **where** to place a student **in each subject area** is the greater concern of the **Curriculum Concept** teachers. "Already knowing some of the standards" is simply a non-issue for the **Lahr-Well Curriculum Concept**, because students (from early entrance K4 through grade 12) move at their own individual paces … no matter the grade level … no matter the basic or advanced subject area. **Only** through testing and daily class-work evaluation will a teacher be able to determine **where** students **are and where** they are **ready to go**."

While the **L-WCC does** have a fundamental curriculum foundation (as listed in the **Progression of Subjects** chart), the **L-WCC** never adopted the **Common Core State Standards**; therefore, it never had the expense of initially adopting, nor the expense, nor legal need to take an oppositional position against because Common Core **never was … is not …** and **never will be** a part of the **Lahr-Well Curriculum Concept**. The **L-WCC** standards **far exceed** those of Common Core. Similar in concept to the Suzuki method in music, students in schools implementing the **Lahr-Well Curriculum Concept** would be able to transfer from Oregon to Idaho to Florida to New York, and "never miss a step" in their educational process because **all** students in each of the 4 "Levels" Level I: (equal to K4 through 1st grade); Level II: (equal to

ALMEDA M. LAHR-WELL, Ph.D.

2nd through 5th grades); Level III: (equal to 6th through 8th grades); and Level IV: (equal to 9th through 12th grades), move together as a class in the natural sciences, the social sciences, robotics and engineering, the fine arts, music history, and 5 foreign languages, **while** moving independently in basic skills development. Basic facts, including vocabulary in **every** subject area, are **repeated each year while** students expand … at their own pace … in each subject area.

Delisle eventually turns from the curricula question of "already knowing" to the fact that … as of the publication of *Dumbing Down America* in 2014, "Four states have yet to adopt the CCSS, with concerns regarding everything from potential costs, to questionable effectiveness (just because educators *say* the CCSS will raise achievements, what proof do they have?)"[29]

However, while 46 states **initially** adopt the 2009 Common Core State Standards, by 2019, **all 50** states have taken strong oppositional positions. Here is what is happening in those states:

(From Thomas More Law Center with active, accessible Website/Facebook pages as of April 15, 2019)

Alabama: Alabamians United for Excellence in Education: Stop Common Core in Alabama,

Alaska: Alaskans Against Common Core

Arizona: Arizonans Against Common Core

Arkansas: Arkansas Against Common Core

California: Californians United Against Common Core CUACC

Colorado: Parents and Educators Against Common Core Curriculum in Colorado

Connecticut: Connecticut Against Common Core

Delaware: Delaware Against Common Core

Florida: Stop Common Core Southeast Florida/Florida Stop Common Core Coalition/Florida Parents R.I.S.E./Opt Out Orlando/Moms Against Duncan/Floridians Against Common Core/Florida Citizens' Alliance

Georgia: Stop Common Core in Georgia/Georgians to Stop Common Core

Hawaii: Stop common Core in Hawaii

Idaho: Idahoans Against Common Core

Illinois: Stop Common Core in Illinois

Indiana: Hoosiers Against Common Core

Iowa: Stop Common Core in Iowa/Concerned Women for America/Iowa

Kansas: Kansans Against Common Core

Kentucky: Kentuckians Against Common Core

Louisiana: Stop Common Core in Louisiana/Parents and Educators Against Common Core Curriculum in Louisiana

Maine: No Common Core in Maine

Maryland: Stop Common Core in Maryland/Marylanders Against Common Core

Massachusetts: Stop Common Core in Massachusetts

Michigan: Stop Common Core in Michigan

Minnesota: Minnesotans Against Common Core

Mississippi: Stop Common Core in Mississippi

Missouri: Missouri Coalition Against Common Core

Montana: Montanans Against Common Core

Nebraska: Nebraska Family Forum

Nevada: Stop Common Core Nevada

New Hampshire: Stop Common Core in New Hampshire

New Jersey: The Committee to Combat Common Core Curriculum

New Mexico: NM Refuse the Tests

New York: Stop Common Core in New York/Stop Common Core in New York State

North Carolina: Stop Common Core NC

North Dakota: Stop Common Core in North Dakota

Ohio: Ohioans Against Common Core

Oklahoma: Stop Common Core in Oklahoma/Restore Oklahoma Public Education

Oregon: Oregon Save Our Schools/Stop Common Core in Oregon/Parents Rights in Education

Pennsylvania: Pennsylvanians Against Common Core

Rhode Island: Stop Common Core in RI

South Carolina: Stop Common Core in South Carolina/South Carolina Parents Involved in Education

South Dakota: South Dakotans Against Common Core

Tennessee: Tennessee Against Common Core

Texas: Concerned Women for America/Women in the Wall/Texans Against SCOPE

Utah: Utahans Against Common Core

Vermont: Stop Common Core in VT

Virginia: Virginians Concerned about K-12 Education

Washington: Stop Common Core in Washington State

West Virginia: WV Against the Common Core

Wisconsin: Stop Common Core in Wisconsin

Wyoming: Wyoming Against the Common Core/Wyoming Citizens Opposing Common Core

According to Accountability Works: A Pioneer Institute and American Principles Project White Paper: *National Cost of Aligning States and Localities to the Common Core Standards* (No. 82 February 2012), had the Common Core Standards been fully implemented in the 50 U.S. states, the projected 7 year cost of implementation and operation would have been (best guesstimate!) $15,835,121,347! (That's almost $16 billion dollars!) This would have been added to the already existing cost of nearly $80 billion for Common Core as reported in January 27, 2016 by Joy Pullmann in *The Federalist*. Now we are nearing $100 billion for nothing! This ... added to the wasted time of building the program, passing the program through state legislatures, the adoption time in 46 states, and then the reversal time in all 50 states cost an unprecedented amount of tax-payer dollars! (Reading *The Long War and Common Core,* you will be given one perspective of **why** this has happened!)

And more generations of U.S. students are lost!

Yet, let us ask, also, **how** did this happen? **Imagine!!! … almost 100 billion dollars!!!**

What sensible, responsible business owner would pay 100 billion dollars for NOTHING? Or, perhaps, the question should be **…** What sensible, responsible business owner **competing in U.S. free enterprise could afford** to pay $100 billion dollars … **for NOTHING?**

How many U.S. corporations could survive this kind of budget fiasco … let alone budget fiasco after fiasco after fiasco? How many U.S. households could survive a comparable budget fiasco? How many of us would believe that, had U.S. education been a competitive "business" of producing "quality" students, instead of the tax-protected empire it is--frequently **producing "failed" products (students)**, that after all of the dollars invested, the new trends, fashions and fads constantly implemented--**with failing results**, and having **exorbitantly "shortchanged"** millions of customers (students **and** their parents) **would STILL BE IN BUSINESS TODAY** … in the free market of these United States?

And yet still more generations of U.S. students are lost!

But the craziness doesn't stop there! In 2009, the *Race to the Top* initiative is created by **President Barack Obama** and Arne Duncan, the ninth U.S. Secretary of Education. This **newest** initiative, abbreviated R2T, RTTT, or RTT, is a **$4.35 billion** U.S. Department of Education **competitive grant**. It is created to spur and reward state and local district K-12 educational innovation and reforms. And while the **Lahr-Well Curriculum Concept** never embraces RTT, that program (RTT), along with most other U.S. educational trends, fashions and fads, does not last long, nor does it have notable results. In 2015 the program is already coming to an end.

And more generations of U.S. students are lost!

While the **Lahr-Well Curriculum Concept** has never implemented the *Race to the Top* initiative, which was supposed to create new models to personalize learning for students, and to help students engage their interests and take responsibility for their success, **the Lahr-Well Curriculum Concept has personalized learning** for **all** students ("tailored" curriculum), in which it also **engages each and every** student in his/her own interests, **in addition to** emphasizing student responsibility for his/her own success.

In his 2014 *Dumbing Down America: The War on Our Nation's Brightest Young Mind,* Delisle suggests … *What We Can Do To Fight Back.* In the 2010 decade, and in this *"Passionate Call to Fix America's School Systems,"* Delisle focuses attention on how gifted children are being shortchanged by a nation that believes smart kids will succeed on their own. **Delisle** makes a convincing plea to address the needs of our U.S. gifted children. He lays out an intriguing call for **three reasons** to care. For his **first reason** he speaks of fourth grade student **Jeff** who, on the first day of school, when asked what he would like to learn, replies to his teacher, "Nuclear physics," offering as a reason: "because his third grade teacher didn't understand it."[30] Delisle goes on to point out that by ninth grade, Jeff's GPA is under 1.0; nuclear physics is only a memory; and Jeff leaves school forever as he turns 16.

Jeff was not challenged or supported early in his education in building the foundation that would have been needed for him to succeed. **Such is not the case with the Lahr-Well Curriculum Concept** where students, as young as 6 years of age, begin drilling with multiplication and division facts. While it may take a student two or three years to pass the entire series of math-facts exams, once these students have passed the 9-10 levels of addition, subtraction, multiplication, division tests, each year the students must pass each of those tests again. Usually with each year, the test accomplishments happen earlier and earlier in the year. Eventually it will take only 10 days (2 weeks) to pass all the required exams … while still moving on in algebra, geometry, pre-trigonometry or …

With the **Lahr-Well Curriculum Concept**, should a student profess a sincere interest in learning an academic subject (as did Jeff), teachers will immediately begin tailoring a curriculum that will not only build the basic skills required with the curriculum itself, but a curriculum that will address the student at his/her beginning abilities, with the intent of building on those abilities, at an exceptional speed, to take the student where he/she would like to go! A child **has never been lost** with the **L-WCC** because a teacher did not understand a subject. With the **L-WCC**, that student's needs are met … **even if** it means "bringing on board" **one teacher** to teach that particular subject to that **one student**!

Delisle's **2ⁿᵈ reason** is represented in his case on female **class valedictorian Morgan**, and her disappointing high school experience with her AP classes, lamenting how much material was **not** covered, and the manner in which the **limited** material **was** presented. He goes on to share Morgan's view that:

"[T]he glowing sense of victory I had always expected to show up at high school graduation had stood me up."[31]

Delisle's **3ʳᵈ reason** is **Justin**, an 18-year-old college freshman, whom earlier in his "traditional" education had been labeled by many of his teachers as an "underachiever" with ADHD. He eventually drops out of college and later shares, **"what can you achieve in an environment where you are not challenged and lose interest quickly?"[32]** Justin recalled the prelude to this position, as early as kindergarten when the teacher, knowing that Justin could read (an inconvenience for many districts, as well as kindergarten teachers), forced Justin to study the alphabet. Justin's final words on his "traditional" education were …

"I'm full of questions about life, not just some material I'm supposed to memorize from a textbook. I craved some connection and didn't get it. I guess you could say I'm searching for a purpose—that is what drives me and, when I find it, it will guide me."[33]

Such is not the case with the **Lahr-Well Curriculum Concept** of **Synergistic Academics** where neither the administration nor the teachers are allowed to "label" students. When records of transfer on a student are received, where special learning challenges are discussed, those records **are not reviewed**, nor are those records shared with the faculty--**until** a period of about two weeks has passed where the faculty has had an opportunity to observe and respond without being influenced by someone else's label. For **Lahr-Well Academy** staff who implement the **L-WCC, labeling a child does not help**. It is our "job" to test and to **discover where** the **challenges and/or gifts** are **for each student**. **Then it becomes our responsibility to reduce and/or eliminate the challenges, as well as to fortify the gifts!**

ALMEDA M. LAHR-WELL, Ph.D.

How unfortunate for Justin, Morgan and Jeff (as it has been--and **is**--for hundreds of thousands/ millions of other **children who have been lost** within "traditional" education), that they did not have an **opportunity to experience the Lahr-Well Curriculum Concept/SA** where memorization of facts, while still an integral part of the curriculum, is **used to connect every** aspect of study within the Concept.

While U.S. teachers passed through a time of, more or less, 125 years **rewriting** "traditional" education, the last four or five decades of eliminating "boring" memorization of facts (the multiplication tables), and cursive writing, have resulted in "throwing out the baby with the bathwater." **Why** would educators decide that learning these foundational math facts would be **boring** or **nonessential**? **Have not** enough of these educators ordered from a fast-food employee who, when the cash register "goes down," was not (**is not**) able to make change? Have these educators not heard of professional exams where applicants are not allowed the use of calculators? Will mothers and fathers have to "sign on the line" for home loans, car purchases, or signature verifications … for their **adult** children who no longer know cursive writing?

And yet more generations of students are lost!

Delisle closes with "No Child Left Behind forgot one vital group: gifted kids."[34] I, on the other hand, believe that NCLB left behind 4 groups of "kids" … academically-at-risk, learning-disabled, average and gifted!

One of the **Lahr-Well** "promises" is that if your child is not gifted when he/she enters **LAW**, he/she **will be** on **graduation day … 12th grade**! The premise of this **Lahr-Well Curriculum Concept** promise is that **because** there should be **NO-ONE-SIZE-FITS-ALL** in education, **those** hundreds of thousands of gifted, average, learning-disabled, as well as academically-at-risk children … not only are **not left behind**, they are **all given what they need to excel**!

The **L-WCC** bases each child's learning program on this premise. For this sole reason, each child (academically-at-risk, learning-disabled, average, and gifted) has an individualized, tailored program built on developing personal, basic skills, while providing a learning environment mixture of audial, oral, visual and kinesthetic approaches that cover the spectrum of learning. While this approach "plays to" the learning-approach strengths of a student, it also continually strengthens any weaknesses which might be more challenging for the student.

Building strengths, eliminating weaknesses, connection **and** purpose **are** all **critical** to the **Lahr-Well Curriculum Concept of Synergistic Academics**. While some traditional curriculums teach … **thematic** units, the **entire L-WCC** K4 through grade 12, intentionally ties reading to math to science to art to music to history to patriotism to every academic subject included within the **Curriculum**. The **Curriculum** prepares students for local, national and global leadership roles--with focuses on the U.S. Constitution, International Governments, and Global Economies.

CHAPTER IX

Still A Nation at Risk

It is 2002, and the *No Child Left Behind Act* is passed into law. Margaret Spelling, later to be U.S. Secretary of Education, has helped create … and becomes a principal proponent of *NCLB*. She tells the nation that the Act "commits" our schools to bringing all students up to grade level or better in reading and math by 2014.

Six years later (2008) Margaret Spelling states in *A Nation Accountable*, the U.S. Department of Education's 25-year retrospective on the impact of *A Nation at Risk*, that "we remain a nation at risk, but are also now a nation informed, a nation accountable, and a nation that recognizes there is much work to be done…"[35]

NCLB has now been in its implementation from 2002-2013. Actually, it had expired in 2007, but Congress never authorizes a replacement. *NCLB* stays in effect. It is now 2014, and the U.S. education system has been declared "At Risk" for more than 40 years. (Just imagine for how many decades education had been deteriorating **before** this declaration!) Delisle references *NCLB* as "a sad reminder of good intentions gone bad."[36] And where are we almost 40 years later? We are **still A Nation at Risk!** Decades of statistics have continued to uncover how much further and further behind we find ourselves in global, educational achievement!

And yet more generations of U.S. students are lost!

So, more than 40 years of statistics, charts, graphs and reports continue to expose U.S. education's demise. However, those "in charge" continue to camouflage the crises. They insist on offering "new," even more damaging, **unproven** "solutions" that are "thrown against the wall to see what will stick"!

As **Delisle** continues comparing the U.S. educational results with those of other nations, he quotes Gregory **Ferenstein (2012)**, a critic of some of the international school comparisons, who states: "Since international comparisons began in 1964, the United States has *never* led the pack."[37] And although this supposedly is a **defense** of U.S. test statistics (because in the U.S. we test **everybody**), for me, it ironically "plays more" to the reality of the U.S. falling further, and further, and further behind in **both** international **and** national test results in math, reading and English! Delisle adds, "To be sure, the United States needs to prop up its educational standards for **any** child for whom the bar is set too low …"[38] (This author's emphasis)

Indeed, the U.S. **did and does** need to prop up its educational standards, in general, for **every** child! So, to whom do we turn to accomplish this seemingly impossible task? To whom have we turned in the decades past--after *A Nation at Risk* first appears? Who is it that has been continually asked to "turn the system around"? Too many times over the last 40 years the "fix-it-gurus" have come **from inside the system** … the "gurus" who created the crises to begin with!

Is this what U.S. business and industry do? Is this what Chrysler did when it was "going under"? **NO!** Chrysler brought in an outsider … Lee Iacocca … someone who could see "the forest **and** the trees" … someone who "turned the company around" … not only financially, but ideologically as well! Out of the ashes of destruction rose the **new Chrysler Corporation!**

So, would it not seem reasonable to look for someone **outside the U.S. education system** to "turn the crises around" … **someone** who has some**thing** that embraces "the forest **and** the trees"?

Look no further! The **something** is here! The **something** is the **Lahr-Well Curriculum Concept of Synergistic Academics!** **This** concept offers not only an ideological curriculum solution, but a financial solution as well! (**Right here in River City** … aka Edwardsville, IL … for those too young to remember *The Music Man!*)

Indeed, the **L-WCC/SA** raises the bar for **every** child … academically-at-risk, learning-disabled, average, and gifted, as well! The **LWCC/SA** is structured so that **every** child is challenged in **every** subject … with additional subjects, often not part of a "traditional" education, included! This **living and breathing Curriculum** has been developed, and is constantly updated, to offer, not only a foundational education (from K4 through grade 12) in **conventional** American history, as well as all of the subjects listed in the **Progression Chart**.

To evaluate this **Progression of Curriculum**, nationally-standardized tests are administered 3 times yearly, at **every** grade level. Tests are **never** taught. With the **L-WCC**, tests are constantly administered in order for the teachers to "keep their fingers on every child's educational pulse." This results in a constant, critical self–examination of the **Curriculum** and those who administer it.

Delisle suggests, "Secondary-level students need more than just harder content in high school classes --they also need to experience the world beyond high school."[39]

The Lahr-Well Curriculum Concept has implemented this idea since its beginnings more than 35 years ago. It provides those experiences, not just for high school students, but for **all** students. Every year the **L-WCC** gives **every** student 10 to 12 field trips, in an effort to try to offer professional interaction with students, as well as to enlighten students about the world surrounding them. This is highlighted through trips such as the professionally-led archaeological dig at Cahokia Mounds State Park where students not only interact with professional archaeologists, but also learn about the actual sight and the "part it played" in the history of our great country.

Instead of field trips, **Delisle** mentions the possibility of virtual academies which he states have actually existed since 1929. **Delisle** views these as engaging "gifted kids." However, in this reference, he asks,

> How could a school that graduates 20 kids a year possibly offer calculus or British Literature? And even if there were a bunch of teens ready to tackle *Paradise Lost* … would there be any teacher in town knowledgeable and qualified enough to teach the course?[40]

The Lahr-Well Curriculum Concept has already addressed these issues: One of the key tenets of the Curriculum Concept is that **one-size-does-not-fit-all**. Calculus is offered, even if only to one student at a time, and full notes and tests have already been written for the 272 *World Literary Masterpieces* and the 80 *World Philosophy* pieces. These notes and tests can be used to teach the teacher at the same time as teaching the student!

An additional advantage of the **L-WCC** over a virtual academic course of study is **real** teachers interacting with **real** students dealing with **real issues,** no matter how small or large the class size (maximum 15). It's amazing how much educational growth occurs when actually exchanging conversational thoughts!

Delisle asks, "Who among the intellectual elite decided that a one-size-fits-all approach to education is appropriate?"[41] And, although, in general, I agree with Delisle, I must acknowledge that, **to some degree**, there is a need for an educational foundation **of some kind!** The challenge is to balance the academic foundation with the academic superstructure!

It is imperative that flights of fancy be encouraged … to keep a student's dreams alive, but the student must also have the basic information he or she needs to build the rocket/space ship that will take him or her to those unimaginable heights! **The Lahr-Well Curriculum Concept of Synergistic Academics achieves** this!

Delisle goes on to ask if **everyone could be gifted? Absolutely** … (with an IQ of about 90 and above)! That is a pretext under which the **L-WCC** operates. In fact, **Lahr-Well Academy** offers in its brochure: "If your child is not gifted when he or she enters, he or she **will be** on the day of high school graduation." The **Academy** can offer this because "gifted" has such an expansive definition that it includes the fact that **every** person has, at least, one gift (if not many gifts). And it is the Academy's teaching staff's task … through oral, aural, visual, and kinesthetic learning approaches to find and enhance each child's gift/s, as well as to find and rectify each child's deficiencies. This is accomplished with the combined foundational and tailored curriculum, as well as the teachers' implementation, **and** the teaching-team work.

Delisle again addresses *No Child Left Behind.* Once again, I reflect on his comment about *NCLB* … being nothing but a sad reminder … words that suggest its actual demise:

> Although NCLB will soon be nothing but a sad reminder of good intentions gone bad, its implementation from 2002-2013 hampered the learning of millions of gifted kids nationwide—and may continue to do so in years ahead.[42]

And so more generations of "kids," not only "gifted," but average, learning-disabled, and academically-at-risk as well **are left behind!**

ALMEDA M. LAHR-WELL, Ph.D.

And more generations of students are lost!

However, working from the position (in **L-WCC**) that **every** child could be **"gifted"** automatically embraces *No Child Left Behind* as well as addresses Delisle's concern in *Dumbing Down America: The War on Our Nation's Brightest.*

However, **Delisle** insists that he is not ready to leave the quagmire of *No Child Left Behind* and the "one-size-fits-all" approach and its costly failures. He suggests that *NCLB* was the perfect storm--bad logic coupled with bad practice: Soon when students were not earning "proficiencies," the test score passing rates were simply lowered, **or** new assessments designed, **or** students were taught the tests, **or** cheating was allowed, **or** administrators began to "fudge" numbers. (This author's emphasis)

The test scores eventually meant nothing. Education "leaders" enhanced their district images through false data, and **parents "bought it … hook, line and sinker" … and are still "buying it" today!**

Of course, this was going to happen! Why didn't educators "figure this out" beforehand? One-size will-**never-**fit-all! **Common sense** tells us this when we order clothes--even socks! We **know** that one size sock doesn't fit all! **Why** would we "assume" that one-size-education would "fit all"?

NCLB that was directed at bringing children up to a "level playing field," in and of itself, automatically left gifted children behind. We know, as adults, that to ignore … or hold back … "gifted" students … until everyone (or almost everyone) catches up, is to thwart great opportunities of creative, problem-solving to individuals and to society.

Delisle continues: "Compounding the problem, individual states began to cut back on gifted services."[43] … These misdirected efforts of NCLB, where test performance was the single criterion by which success was judged, resulted in a watered-down curriculum that focused on a limited range of topics.[44]

Every new decade seems to bring about the next-great-wave of educational-reform. The **Progressive Education** movement of the 1930s attempted to turn teachers into social reformers. The **Back to Basics** movement of the 1950s (and revisited by many states in the 1990s) emerged in response to students' (supposed) inability to master even simple facts. The "**open classrooms**" of the 1960s-1970s found schools being constructed without interior walls, while its critics contended that a touchy feely, student-centered classroom lacked rigor, discipline, and consistency. **Tracking by academic ability … a whole language approach to literacy … a constructivist approach** to teach mathematics organically … best-selling books edited by E. D. Hirsch asserting in excruciating detail what every first or second or third grader should know … all popular reforms at one time or another.

Ay yi yi! Can we handle any more reforms? Ready or not, here one comes: for 21st century learners, it's differentiated instruction.

Actually, in theory, differentiated instruction is the strategic bedrock on which the foundation of gifted education rests. Essentially, differentiation takes a look at several factors:

- *what* students know already and what they still need to learn (content),

- *how* students can demonstrate their knowledge (process),

- *what* evidence students provide that documents their learning (product), and

- *where* and *under what conditions* students go about learning (environment).[45]

(This author's bolding)

Delisle, seemingly frustrated, suggests that there continues to be no shortage of the **next best, greatest U.S. educational programs.** Yet scores continued (**and continue**) to fall.

And more generations of U.S. students are lost!

Delisle wants to believe that this *NCLB* system, in theory, sounds perfect for students with disabilities (and could sound perfect, as well, for the gifted students), but says,

> in practice, it is harder to implement in a classroom than it is to juggle with one arm tied behind your back … [b]ecause those who promote differentiation – and school administrators and education professors … particularly fond of doing so – will argue that if a school has a differentiation mindset, there is no need for specific gifted programs. The logic goes that if *all* teachers are challenging *all* students by offering differentiated lessons to *all* kids, then supplementary, out-of-classroom services for students who excel are redundant. Why 'pull out' kids with gifted abilities when you can 'pull them in' to a differentiated classroom and reach the same ends? The trouble is, those ends are seldom reached.[46]

My answer to "those ends are seldom reached," is, **Yes and No** … with the **L-WCC/SA**, those ends are **always reached** … unless a student were to absolutely refuse to move forward! When Delisle states that if a school were to have a differentiation mindset, there would be no need for specific gifted programs, **that is exactly what the L-WCC does.** As students move together in **some** subject areas, **all** students are provided what they need to move faster, and more in-depth, in subjects … especially where they are "gifted." The **L-WCC always finds** ways to either "pull out" or "provide within the established structure," ways of challenging **all** students **above and beyond!**

Delisle demands, "Don't hold back! If a 10-year-old is ready for a calculus class, arrange it for her. Other than a minimum legal age for some activities, services, or privileges, age never matters as much as it does in school. Age and ability are not a required match in real-world applications of giftedness."[47]

This is a central premise of **the L-WCC/SA** … to **never hold back** a child! If a 10-year-old is ready for a calculus class, the Academy director arranges **a calculus class for one student**. That opportunity is offered to **each and every student! Excellence in academic education is the Lahr-Well Curriculum Concept** where a child … **every** child … **is provided the tools needed to succeed! With the L-WCC, students progress at an accelerated rate consistent with their abilities … not their ages.** A child should **never** be "held back" academically … for any reason … let alone, due to his/her age! A child learns to

ALMEDA M. LAHR-WELL, Ph.D.

reach for the goal placed before him/her. To tell a child not to "reach for the stars" is to shackle that child to mediocrity … very likely … for the rest of his/her life!

For those credentialed persons who take the position that such acceleration causes social and emotional harm to children, they ignore the losses of hundreds of thousands (millions) of students who become "bored" and "turned off" to "traditional" education. As Einstein is quoted, **"Great spirits have always encountered violent opposition from mediocre minds."** (This author's emphasis) Take into consideration Mozart, Einstein, or Aretha Franklin! What did "traditional" schools do with these brilliant students?

Nationally-standardized test scores prove that **L-WCC/SA has been (and is)** consistently, and amazingly successful with, virtually, **all** students … (combining foundational with tailored curriculum). Yet, anything **equal to** this **Concept**, to my knowledge, **did not exist** (and **does not exist** today) in U.S. education … except for the **Lahr-Well Academy**'s **Lahr-Well Curriculum Concept of Synergistic Academics!**

CHAPTER X

The Degradation of U.S. History in School Textbooks

According to Donna H. Hearne, in *The Long War and Common Core: Everything You Need to Know to Win the War*,

> *The Long War and Common Core* is a comprehensive history of Common Core's background, which has roots that stretch more than a hundred years back. It is called Common Core today, but will soon be renamed, just as what happened with Progressive Education, Mastery Learning, Moral Relevancy/No Absolutes, Outcome Based Education, America 2000, Goals 2000, and No Child Left Behind. Common Core is the latest effort by a progressive, autocratic elite to completely *transfer all decisions* concerning children from parents, teachers, and school boards to themselves, and to completely *transform America* from a nation of responsible, moral, independent human beings endowed by their Creator with unalienable rights of life, liberty and the pursuit of happiness to robots and servants of the state.[48]

Hearne goes on to explain:

> **We are in a war ... not just a battle**, and Common Core is the latest campaign that is the current front line of this war. It follows previous skirmishes in the 1930s over Progressive Education, the 1950s over Secular Humanist Education, and more recently in the 1990s over Outcome Based Education. All of these strategies are based on the premise of 'progressive experts,' instead of mom, dad and the teacher, setting common standards for all children. And since these secular, utopian standards drive the curriculum and assessments, local control of education ceases to be a reality.[49]

At this point parents begin losing total control over what their children are to be taught.

Hearne continues:

> In order to change a free nation into a captive nation, you need to control the minds of the next generation – through the schools and culture. Italian communist Antonio Gramsci called it *'the long march through culture,'* in other words, *cultural Marxism sold through the schools, media, and culture ... **the long war.*** This produces a generation hostile to freedom while rendering them unprotected against an enemy intent on conquering the free world with a[n] ideology antagonistic to freedom.
>
> ...
>
> From the Soviet-infiltrated Frankfurt School and Italian communist Antonio Gramsci, to social justice/Marxists William (Bill) Ayers*, the plan was formed to turn America from freedom and liberty to a totalitarian oligarchy through the schools and culture. Adding further anti-Christian dimensions was evolutionist Charles Darwin and secular humanist/socialist John Dewey and his cohorts at Columbia University Teacher's College, while Marxist Howard Zinn's, *A People's History of the United States,* helped destroy the memory of American exceptionalism and brought social justice (renamed, Marxism) into the classroom.[50]

Hearne describes Gramsci as an Italian Marxist theoretician and politician, and Bill Ayers as "one of the communist/socialist radicals who tried to take over the United States through open revolution in the streets in the 1960s."[51]

Now the U.S. educational system embraces a "one-size-fits-all" anti-patriotic American history K through grade 12 ... and beyond ... through 4 years of college.

And more generations of U.S. students are lost, through academics, to a socialist-government concept.

Hearne continues:

> These revolutionary educational movers, movements, and ideas coalesced in 1965, when President Lyndon Johnson created and passed, as a part of the 'war on poverty,' the *Elementary and Secondary Education Act* even through it was not one of the legal areas for federal program, specified in the Constitution. This law cleverly authorized federally-funded education programs, administered by the states, effectively shifting decision-making from the local to the federal. In 2002, congress amended ESEA and reauthorized it as the *No Child Left Behind Act.*[52]

And more generations of U.S. students are lost … as well as any local, political control over "traditional" U.S. education.

Hearne saw, already 5 years ago, what was (and is) happening inside U.S. culture today. **The "revolutionary education movements" … a result of The Frankfurt School's philosophy and decades of its indoctrination, along with the U.S. educational embracing of anti-American … American history textbooks: K through college … laid the foundation for the "cancellation culture" of today … and the effort … not to simply rewrite … but to destroy American history.**

This premonition was also obvious to Michael **Minnicino** who authors an article on The Frankfurt School. Hearne quotes Minnicino from his article titled, "The Frankfurt School and 'Political Correctness'." In it Minnicino suggests that "the concept of the human soul was undermined by the most vociferous intellectual campaign …"[53] Hearne adds that Minnicino states:

> It has brought us to the point that we will have to face the fact that the ugliness we see around us has been consciously fostered and organized in such a way, that a majority of the population is losing the cognitive ability to transmit to the next generation, the ideas and methods upon which our civilization was built.[54]

Hearne confirms Minnicino's thoughts:

> The single, most important organizational component of this conspiracy was a Communist thinktank, called the Institute for Social Research (I.S.R.) [*Institut für Sozialforschung*], but popularly known as the Frankfurt School.[55]

It is The Frankfurt School (better known as Critical Theory, a sociological movement … morphing from Frankfurt School to the 1960s Goethe University Frankfurt … receiving the epithet of "Karl Marx University"), that in 1914, espoused their "political movement could only succeed when the individual believes that his or her actions are determined by not a personal destiny, but the destiny of the community in a world that has been abandoned by God."[56]

This begins to "take hold" in the 1980s in U.S. elementary, secondary, and post-secondary schools and universities via **Marxist Howard Zinn's** *A People's History of the United States* textbook. Virtually adopted, nationally, as **the** American history textbook, it dramatically, catastrophically changes American history for **generations** of American students. On the foundation of what Marxists had already built, Zinn's American history continues to "indoctrinate" … according to **Hearne** … "by omission."

> Much of the history of Western civilization's great inventors, writers, artists, statesmen and scientists steeped in the absolute truths of the Bible is missing, being replaced with modern moral relativists. American history favors Marxist Howard Zinn's heroes, not Paul Revere, John Adams, Ben Franklin, and Thomas Edison. The focus is on envy and class warfare. Even the innovation of hospitals and children's homes in the late nineteenth century by

ALMEDA M. LAHR-WELL, Ph.D.

progressives such as the Roosevelt family does not receive their due. By ignoring certain things such as the rise of private Christian philanthropy, the student cannot include this as an option to solve a problem, since he knows nothing about it.[57]

Hearne continues to make her case on the damages of Zinn's anti-American history text:

By simply not mentioning certain subjects … totalitarian propagandists have influenced opinion much more effectively than they could have done by the most … compelling of logical rebuttals.[58]

A nation that does not know where it came from will never know where it is going. Today, our nation does not realize how close we are to Adolph Huxley's *Brave New World* where man is reduced to a robot, existing only for the use of a self-appointed cadre of progressive utopians and where each child has already been identified through massive data sorting and selection to meet the *greater good*. While American policy in education has historically focused on reading, writing and arithmetic, progressive/materialistic revisionists have claimed the high ground in historic re-interpretation, especially of American history and have been removing the underpinnings of what makes America free.[59]

Could **Hearne** possibly be referring, again, to Howard **Zinn**'s *A People's History of the United States* which has been adopted throughout the United States, especially at the high school level, to replace **"conventional"** history? Do you not wonder, *"What happened?"*, when you see young people (late teens/ early twenties) who cannot name the first president of the United States … let alone the **16th** president? (Lincoln) … Do you not wonder *"What has happened?"* when college students, interviewed on the streets, cannot name the country/power against whom the colonists fought?

Howard **Zinn**'s *A People's History of the United States* (1980) has been adopted as **the** high school history text throughout the nation! It seems to offer moving information about "America's women, factory workers, African-Americans, Native Americans, the working poor, and immigrant laborers."[60] But as the author progresses from Columbus to Clinton, he highlights multitudes of travesties and travails of the "American people" … at the hands of the American white male. And while the aforementioned groups' losses clearly did and do merit addressing, Zinn's history book does not even begin to "paint the picture" of the invaluable contributions of the American heroes who sacrificed great losses to help build this land of the free and home of the brave.

As **Zinn** talks about the land greed of great American heroes like Washington and Jefferson, he does not mention the merits of what either of these men did for their country. **Zinn** moves throughout the rest of U.S. History, in the same vein. When he speaks about Lincoln, **Zinn** paints a negative picture:

Hence, it was Abraham Lincoln who freed the slaves, not John Brown. In 1859, John Brown was hanged, with federal complicity, for attempting to do by small-scale violence what Lincoln would do by large-scale violence several years later—end slavery.[61]

In fact, in the few pages where Lincoln **is** addressed in Zinn's book, while numerous negatives are pointed out, the *Gettysburg Address*, acclaimed as one the greatest U.S. presidential speeches ever written, as well as a speech that would reunite a war-torn nation … is never mentioned!

When **Zinn** writes about 911, under Afghanistan … not under the U.S., he writes:

> Nine months into his (George W. Bush) presidency, on September 11, 2001 … hijackers on three different planes flew the huge jets, loaded with fuel, into the twin towers of the World Trade Center in downtown New York, and into one side of the Pentagon in Washington, D.C. As Americans all over the country watched, horrified, they saw on their television screens the towers collapse in an inferno of concrete and metal, burying thousands of workers and hundreds of firemen and policemen who had gone to their rescue.
>
> It was an unprecedented assault against enormous symbols of American wealth and power undertaken by 19 men from the Middle East, most of them from Saudi Arabia. They were willing to die in order to deliver **a deadly blow against what they clearly saw as their enemy, a superpower that had thought itself invulnerable.**[62] (This author's emphasis)

Once again, **Zinn** seems to make **heroes of the 19 men** (later declared U.S. terrorists), and **villain of the United States**. In fact, **Zinn** also presents the U.S. as aggressor in the bombings of Hiroshima and Nagasaki, and omits numerous U.S. presidents, as well as Neil Armstrong, Einstein, John Glenn, NASA, Pearl Harbor, Paul Revere, Betsy Ross, the Space Race, etc., etc., etc.

American patriotism is being rejected, slandered, and twisted to the extent that Advanced Placement American history worksheets "have *somehow* left out the Thomas Edisons, Benjamin Franklins, and the rich history of George Washington in favor of social justice."[63]

American high school and college students have been studying Zinn's anti-American perspective for generations now (original publication in 1980) in U.S. "traditional," parochial and private schools. And, not only is **Zinn's** history written with such a negative view of our country and its white male heroes (who all had and have flaws … as do **all of us**), but many U.S. publishing companies have followed suit during this same time. Therefore, it is no wonder that U.S. students no longer embrace … or **even know** our nation's factual history. Additionally, as statistical research continues to expose, general academic, basic skills intentionally are being disposed of in U.S. kindergarten through grade 12 education.

Is it any wonder why the U.S. educational system is in crisis? Is it any wonder now as to **why** our high school and college students have developed what seems to be a *hatred* for this "land of the free and home of the brave"? This possibly gives us some insight into the 2020 Cancellation Culture and riots in …

Atlanta
Boston
Chicago
Columbus

ALMEDA M. LAHR-WELL, Ph.D.

Dallas/Fort Worth

Des Moines

Denver

Detroit

DC

Houston

Los Angeles

Louisville

Memphis

Minneapolis

NYC

Phoenix

Portland

Sacramento

San Jose

This is **not the case** with **the Lahr-Well Curriculum Concept** where **"conventional"** U.S. history is taught, and historical interpretations, such as Zinn's, are referenced as recognized, **alternative** perspectives. **L-WCC** students study from books where **all** the U.S. presidents are listed and where our great men and women heroes are highlighted. Students memorize all the presidents, in sequential order, study the Constitution numerous times during their junior high/senior high years, memorize the Amendments to the Constitution (as well as study them in-depth), memorize the Preamble to the Constitution, as well as the *Gettysburg Address*. Additionally, students learn the historical and philosophical contents of such, and from ages 6 through 18 study and **know** the names of, not only, the most highly-recognized U.S. leaders, but also, *100 Americans Who Shaped American History* (including women and African Americans), *100 Inventions That Shaped World History*, *100 Scientists Who Shaped World History*, *100 Americans Who Shaped American History*, *100 Men Who Shaped World History*, *100 Women Who Shaped World History*, and *100 Natural Wonders of the World* … **every year!**

Many U.S. history textbooks not only diminish and dismiss patriotism now, but actually provoke antagonistic and anarchistic feelings against our Founding Fathers (and Mothers), and the hundreds of thousands of men and women who have suffered and died for our U.S. freedoms. Too many U.S. history textbooks now condemn these American heroes and make acidic apologies for our nation's actions.

Besides the assault on American history, **Hearne** also addresses an assault on literary history in her observations on English Language Standards from Common Core Standards:

> English Language Standards in the Common Core Standards includes this exercise: 'Interpret figures of speech (e.g., literary, biblical, and mythological allusions) in context.' However, most schools are preventing students from reading and studying the Bible, therefore how can they *interpret* a biblical figure of speech? How can they identify the

numerous scriptural passages from the King James Bible in the writings of Shakespeare, George Washington, Samuel Coleridge, and others if they are not familiar with the Bible?

Another section of the standards instructs the student to 'Analyze how an author draws on and transforms source material in a specific work (e.g., how Shakespeare treats a theme or topic from Ovid or the Bible or how a later author draws on a play by Shakespeare.) The allusion behind 'the handwriting is one the wall' has little meaning to students who do not know the biblical story of Daniel and Belshazzar in the fifth chapter of Daniel.[64]

… "Although pornographic literature is not banned in the classroom, the Bible is hard to find with most teachers believing it is off limits."[65]

Once again, **HOW DID THIS HAPPEN???**

Hearne offers her perspective on this by claiming this "remaking" of American (U.S.) history … U.S. education began with the American infiltration of John Dewey and his philosophical/educational cohorts … back in the 1930s.

I, as a university/college instructor/professor for the past 50 years, and as the founder and director of the **Lahr-Well Academy (L-WCCSA)** for the past 35 years, had been under the illusion that U.S. educators had just been "turning a blind eye" to what had been happening since the 1930s; but after having digested Donna Hearne's *The Long War and Common Core*, I have been sadly enlightened as to how significant elements of the U.S. education system and its core of administrators did **not** "turn a blind-eye" to what was happening, **but rather embraced and promoted** what was happening.

I fail to understand why "traditional" education continues to travel down the road of self-destruction. Why had it abandoned phonics, after World War II, when it bore evidence that, no matter what new reading method … reading trend, fashion or fad of the decade was introduced, U.S. reading scores continued to fall? Why did "traditional" education, as a whole, but not all, decide that it was too "boring" to have children memorize … especially to memorize multiplication facts? Why had cursive instruction been "thrown out the window"? And **when** did U.S. college and university students become so anti-American … to the point where students seemingly have begun to "hate" the U.S. as a republic, along with its democratic principles?

Hearne states, "*To change a free nation into a captive nation of robots and zombies, indoctrinate them with what to think instead of teaching them how to think, while removing all moral absolutes.*"[66]

President Reagan had already seen this coming in 1961:

> Freedom is never more than one generation away from extinction. We didn't pass it on to our children in the bloodstream. It must be fought for, protected, and handed on for them to do the same, or one day we will spend our sunset years telling our children and our children's children what it was once like in the United States where [men] were free.[67]

And more generations of U.S. students are lost!

ALMEDA M. LAHR-WELL, Ph.D.

CHAPTER XI

Antidote to Common Core …
The Lahr-Well Difference

Today, opposition to the federal takeover of education (*Common Core)* can come in the form of a private enterprise, a business or industry preparatory school, and/or a military "prep" school. Here, it is called **"The Lahr-Well Difference."**

"Traditional" education has squandered far too many opportunities to break from the gridlock in which generations of students have been caught … and lost! "Preparatory schools," with the 35-year **proven** curriculum of **the Lahr-Well Curriculum Concept of Synergistic Academics is** a way for students to soar into the future!

Understanding the threats to freedom and liberty, we **must** re-establish the strengths of

- freedom and liberty

- Judeo-Christian morals and values

- academic excellence in our K-12 schools, as well as our colleges and universities … and our armed forces!

One way to regain these three key strengths is **the L-WCC/SA** … a **proven** solution. Students, instructed within the guidelines of **the L-WCC/SA**, and instructed for 4-6 years, demonstrate nationally standardized test results 2 to 3 and 5 to 6 years beyond their chronological ages. The differences account for individual learning-abilities (and the amount of desire to learn) among the academically-at-risk, the learning-disabled, the average, and the gifted. The **Curriculum** has not been implemented for behaviorally at-risk; however, it **has** proven itself with mildly-autistic students. The **Curriculum Concept** revolves around

- Curriculum Planning

- Instructional Style

- Meeting the needs of **every** student

- Bringing **each** student to academic excellence

- Helping **each** student to embrace the value of becoming an intelligent, problem-solving, honorable, ethical, patriotic citizen
- Teacher Professional Development
- Student Assessment

I have been asked repeatedly, with all the special curriculum components, if this program is for gifted children only? The answer is a **resounding NO!** The following story explains **why** … and **how!**

In its early years, **Lahr-Well Academy** worked with a young boy who was supposed to be entering 9th grade, but, having been in a "traditional educational environment" through 8th grade, was testing at a low-elementary level in reading, math, and English grammar. He had been placed in the back of the classrooms, given a pencil and paper, and been told to "draw," because he "could not keep up with the class." This young "man" was projected to either drop out of high school, or to graduate one … two … three years late … at the age of 21. He became a student academically "at-risk." In actuality what he needed was a **tailored** curriculum that brought him out of his academic "black hole," and the push to develop a strong sense of self-esteem. He was an amazing young man who has become an amazing, patriotic citizen!

Upon his arrival to **Lahr-Well Academy,** the student would not look us in the eyes when he would speak with us. Of course, his self-esteem had been badly damaged through his previous educational experiences. As with all students, his "tailored curriculum" was immediately developed. Unlike "traditional" educational environments, where students' "IEPs" (Individual Educational Plans) take 3 to 6 months to develop, it takes **5 minutes** (Let me emphasize: **5 minutes**) to develop a **Lahr-Well Curriculum Concept** individualized, tailored curriculum! And once I have developed the individualized (tailored) plan, and it is implemented, it takes the teaching team only 1 to 3 days to "figure out" whether or not the student has been mistakenly placed at a certain level in a subject. The teacher and I visit, and we **immediately** resolve the issue! And while "traditional" educators will most likely say, "Impossible," I will respond, "Come see 'how it's **done**'!"

An aside: We, at the Academy, actually do not allow our students (K4 through grade 12) to say, "It's **done**," unless they are speaking about something being baked in an oven. Otherwise, they must say, "It's **finished**."

As a linguist, words are **critically important** to me. We teach students to be "eager," instead of "anxious" in waiting for an event to occur. It's amazing how this helps students understand that "mere vocabulary" can help them avoid feeling "anxious" in their lives … unless there is something **truly** about which to feel "anxious."

The Academy staff-team works diligently at not letting students **loosely** use the words **love** and **hate.** We work at not letting them say they "love" things … whether that be pizza or a particular type of jeans, and not letting them say they "love to do" something. We work at teaching them to say they "really, really like" material things, or that they really like doing something … but that they should "reserve" the word "love" for people and pets … if it is truly "love" about which they are speaking. We work at teaching them to **love God, Family (pets), and Country … in that order.** We work at teaching them that "love" is **not** a synonym for "like" … hoping to prepare them for more balanced and moderate life choices.

ALMEDA M. LAHR-WELL, Ph.D.

Per team instruction, we work at not allowing students to use the word "hate" at all! There will be those who will contest that the word "hate" is in the Bible, so it is a perfectly "legitimate" word. **However,** I insist that students let that word "stay" in the Bible. Let God have full control of that word. Knowing the sensitive psyche of children and young adults, the teaching-team understands that if children grow up saying they "hate" broccoli or they "hate" reading, it becomes so much easier for them to say to their parents, "I hate you," when parents insist on children following house rules … doing homework, arriving home at a specific time, or to say to another student, or teacher, "I hate you because of … race, ethnicity, religion, or for simply doing something students **think** is unfair. We work diligently at teaching exceptional communication and cooperation skills, while at the same time teaching students to "take a respectful stand" when they feel passionately about something. This way students build their vocabulary while learning to be extremely careful with **the words they choose … and how they choose to express those words**. This teaches **solid** communication skills.

I have digressed! Let us return to our 9th grade student! After developing this young man's tailored program, we began to work on his self-esteem. At that time, it was customary for us to have an annual dinner/dance fund-raiser that featured a skit written to include **each** student in the school. We gave this particular student the lead role. Immediately his mother said, "I don't think he can or will do that." Well, to "make that story short," in as few as 4 short months, not only did the young man bravely embrace the lead role, he looked the audience "in the eye," and projected beautifully! We were all amazed at his transformation!

This transformation continued for 2½ years until the young man was about to go into what would have been his junior year of high school. However, the end of his junior year would have brought about his closest classmate/friend moving to another level outside the Academy, and a group of 6th graders coming into the middle school/high school mix. With there being a 5 to 6-year age difference between this one student and his new 6th grade classmates, we could see a "change of heart" occurring in this young man who would now be the oldest of this mixed group. His self-esteem began to falter … but not for long!

In his 3 years with us, he was to gain (and did gain) 7 years in reading, 5½ years in English, and 5 years in math, and although he was still "just a little" behind, he was very close to senior class competency. However, seeing what the future might bring, I went to our local junior college, with his ACT scores and asked if they would admit this student the following year (his projected, upcoming graduation--one year early from high school) … giving him transitional classes in English and math … if necessary. The junior college replied that his ACT scores made him eligible for entry. So, instead of this "young man" graduating 1, 2, or 3 years late, or "dropping out" of high school, as "traditional" high school had projected, he **graduated one year early**, and began junior college. Upon graduating from the Academy, this young man was immediately hired by a corporation, at an exceptional salary, and, as a patriotic, community servant, eventually taught classes in his own professional field. He became a responsible and dedicated husband and father. His contribution to family and society has been impressive. His success story at **Lahr-Well Academy** is just one of many similar, anecdotal stories; however, there is neither time nor space to share those here.

One might ask, "How did this happen?" The answer is obvious in the manner in which we worked with this student, as well as with **all** of our students, and their individual gifts and deficiencies. We have learned at **Lahr-Well Academy** that if we receive students one year behind, it generally takes us one year to help them "catch up" before they begin to make greater strides beyond their grade level. Similarly, with students two years behind, it generally takes us about two years to help them "catch up" before they begin to put a positive distance between themselves and their U.S. grade-counterparts.

This is only one end of **the Lahr-Well Curriculum Concept of Synergistic Academics** spectrum. In the center are the learning-disabled and average students … and their tailored programs. The learning-disabled and average students tend to achieve grade levels 2 to 3 years beyond chronological age … by the time of their high school graduation. The other end is, of course, the gifted students. These students, after 4 to 6 years' instruction, generally test between 4 to 6 years beyond chronological age. Often times these students graduate 1 to 2 years early; however, in order for them to graduate early, they have to, in their last year at the Academy, take a general studies math or science class on campus at a local university, college, or junior-college and earn an A or B in the class. We do not graduate students early just to "walk the streets." Each student who graduates early **has** to prove entry level, or higher, college work … and initiate college applications.

The idea of early graduation, as an occasional standard, arose from my experience at McKendree College (University), in the late 1970s, where I wrote and directed one of the earliest ESL (English as a Second Language) programs in the United States. We recruited students from Central and South America. More often than not, these students came to us as 15 and 16-year-old students who, after **one** semester/year of English with us, enrolled directly into McKendree. The question soon surfaced: Why would Latin American students be ready for college at the ages of 15 and 16 when students of the U.S.--supposedly a scientifically and technologically advanced nation … hold students back until 17, 18, or 19 years of age before "releasing" them for college/university work?

The answers were multiple. First, U.S. high schools received more tax dollars when they held students longer. Second, U.S. parents were "morphing" into "hovering-helicopter" parents … to the extent that young adults were encouraged **not** to accept responsibilities that were (are) required of adulthood. Third, I sadly learned that our U.S. high school graduates were already beginning to place significantly behind our Latin American students in academic achievement!

This, unfortunately, confirmed what statistics had been saying--that **many** U.S. high school graduates are not socially, emotionally or academically ready for a college or university "experience."

However, graduating from **Lahr-Well Academy**, students are "ready," (and often ready early), in all of those areas for a college or university "experience." **The LWCC/SA** provides for **all** students (ages 4-18) … a combination of textbooks; computer work; desk work (individualized basic skills development); 4 natural sciences (biology, chemistry, earth science, physics); daily science experiments and/or activities; 2 social sciences (world history and American history); world geography; hands-on art (through world history); music appreciation (through world history); composition; research; macro and micro economics; robotics and electronics; macro and micro economics; as well as 5 introductory-level foreign languages. Christian students are taught to memorize the *Lord's Prayer* in all 6 (English included) languages. Students of other faiths are not required this skill. **All** students (from ages 4-18) are required to memorize vocabulary, songs,

ALMEDA M. LAHR-WELL, Ph.D.

and short dialogues in each of the 5 foreign languages. Students are not taught to become bilingual in any of these foreign languages; however, they finish their time at the Academy with impressive foreign language skills, and usually, the interest to have already moved beyond basics in one or more languages.

As mentioned, great emphasis is placed on team-teaching morals, values, ethics, and U.S. patriotism, along with an introductory knowledge of civics. Students are taught to memorize the Preamble to the *U.S. Constitution*, the 27 Amendments, as well as the *Gettysburg Address*. Students are still taught that Washington, Jefferson, Jackson, and Lincoln, along with all of our other U.S. presidents, are recognized as leaders and/or heroes … while acknowledging that they were (and we are) flawed people. We stress the "good ol'-fashioned" ***Golden Rule*** of doing unto others as you would have them do unto you. We also teach that "history is written by the winners," and that there is always additional research that can be done in order to better understand the "other side."

The Lahr-Well Curriculum Concept of Synergistic Academics … antidote to *Common Core* … offers the macro: **Progressive Curriculum Concept** … along with the micro: **every-day** multiple-subjects, vocabulary "sensitivity," to the daily use of a **properly-placed** 3-sided gripper … **with the appropriate indentations** for the correct fisngers and thumb. Additionally, students are constantly reminded to "**sit up straight**," and to "**turn their papers … not their heads**." These tedious teacher-tasks help students with posture, handwriting, and help students avoid early astigmatisms. (The astigmatisms occur when students slouch at their papers, tilting their heads to one side, or the other … right-handed vs. left-handed. Once they tilt their heads, one eye focuses straight down, while the other focuses at an angle. This often causes early astigmatisms.)

What appears as "small" things **cannot be** overlooked! **"Little things mean a lot!"**

The **L-WCC** requires that:

- The administrator always teaches, minimally, one class … so that when a teacher sends a student to the administrator's office, or complains of a student's actions, the administrator will most likely have first-hand experience with the potential issues.

- Classroom sizes **must** be small**.** There should be no more than 15 students to a classroom.

- Classes/classrooms can be all one grade … or can be mixed grades in one level … i.e. Level I: Prekindergarten through Grade 1; Level II: 2nd through 5th grade; Level III: 6th through 8th grade; Level IV: 9th through 12th grade.

With the **L-WCC/SA**, not only do students have to train in the macro, as well as the micro, but **teachers have to do the same!** "Teachers-to-be" are not required to have teaching licensure; however, a bachelor's degree is preferred. In fact, it is generally more helpful to have teachers-to-be who have **not** majored in education (but who are competent in their field of expertise) … because it takes time to "unteach" what potential teachers have been taught in "traditional," college or university education classes. (If "degreed" teachers were the answer, "traditional" education would not have the "unprepared teachers" who now have the extra expense and time required to take even **more** exams to become "qualified.") In fact, it is usually helpful to hire younger college-graduates who have not already "bought into" traditional education, or professionals, outside the field of education, who have the subject skills, and simply need "on-the-job" training … to be taught "how to teach."

L-WCC "teachers-to-be" **must intern** "in-house" at the Academy for one year. (The financial cost to them, while modest, helps them "invest" in themselves, as well as **the Concept**.) They must learn how to team-teach, and they must learn how to most effectively deliver the curriculum. **Teachers must work together … as a TEAM … through all curricula! Math teachers must accept that art is as important as math … which is as important as history … which is as important as science, etc. etc. etc.**

Although some of this may sound unusual to "newcomers" … as well as those more experienced, the "proof is definitely in the pudding"! The proof is in the calm, yet enthusiastic student-environment, comradery, knowledge-base and exceptional achievement scores. In fact, if one were to think this through a bit more, one would soon come to understand that, in the U.S. business world, a corporation that continued in a similar, deteriorating fashion … as has the vast tax empire of education, for more than four hundred years, and continued to produce a **declining product** … at a **greater cost** … that corporation would be "out of business" in a "normal" world. Shareholders would demand change that would produce exceptional results. However, in an educational world where competition has been prohibited for most of 300 years, "business" has been anything but "normal."

Constant assessment is an integral element of **the Lahr-Well Curriculum Concept of Synergistic Academics**. **All s**tudents are tested 3 times yearly with an in-house test to measure reading, English, and math skills. Once each year **all** students are given the *Iowa Basic Test of Skills*. (This year was an exception … due to the Coronavirus Pandemic.) The ITBS is forwarded to the test company for computerized grading. We test frequently in order to "keep our fingers on each student's pulse." The in-house tests generally last only one and one-half hours. The teachers **never view** the test and **never teach** the test … whether it be an "in-house" test or a nationally-standardized test that is computer-scored. Sometimes our in-house test scores will be higher, at the end of the year, than the standardized test scores. Sometimes our in-house scores will be lower. Sometimes our in-house scores will be the same as the nationally standardized test scores. We tell parents that the results always depend on what kind of day a student is having … and whether or not the student has or has not "guessed" well. By any means, we can assure parents that … with 3 tests (**LWA** students have 4 each year) students are testing in the "general" areas of those 3 or 4 scores … and that **tests are only one way of gauging** the students' progress.

With this knowledge in-hand, NOW may be the time for larger businesses **and/or** the military to prepare their own **future personnel** … preparing their own K4 through grade 12 students … by leasing and implementing **the Lahr-Well Curriculum Concept of Synergistic Academics!**

ALMEDA M. LAHR-WELL, Ph.D.

CHAPTER XII

One-Size-Does-Not-Fit-All!

The days of classrooms with 20, 30, 37 students--**supposedly moving at the same pace in all subjects--must come to an end** ... if we are to **rescue** (as opposed to **recover** ... in the sense of a fire-department recovery) **U.S. education and its students!** Even with identical twins, it would be unlikely that both children would be on the same level, at the same time, in the same subjects. So, which child wins? Which loses? Or does someone develop individualized, tailored programs for each child?

Neither children nor adults mature at the same pace physically, mentally, emotionally, socially, or spiritually! **Why** would we think it would be different academically? **One size cannot ... and does not ... fit all!** For example, in a class of 37 fifth graders, **all** 37 students **will not** be at the **same** place ... in the **same** skill ... on the **same** day! So, does the teacher teach to the top, to the average, or to the lowest skill level? **Then**, that teacher will have to make that same decision in **every basic skill** to be taught! How many **more** U.S. students will be left behind in the **one-size-fits-all** system?

An alternative to this system is home-schooling. With the Coronavirus Pandemic ... parents--or grandparents/aunts/uncles/older siblings--**were forced** to take positions of instructing children. Staying home all day with the children, those responsible for instruction were either hopeful about receiving guidance **and assignments** from classroom teachers, or they were frustrated trying to "figure out" how to **actually teach** the children **something**. Unfortunately, for many "instructors" it became a matter of **survival** rather than an achievement of enlightenment.

While homeschooling can be a protective and interesting alternative, one person (parent-teacher) generally does not have the knowledge or expertise to guide his/her child/ren in multiple fields of study ... where **a core** of teachers would be able to do so.

While "virtual" academies may offer unique opportunities, they don't offer a classroom environment where the curricula can be synergistic for everyone, and where students can socialize with one another ... especially in a smaller classroom environment.

While many districts still think "bigger is better," teachers in overloaded classrooms don't have time **to actually teach** students social skills i.e., **how and when** to compromise or **when** to "stand one's ground." Nor does the educational system encourage (nor sometimes even allow) teachers to teach morals, values, ethics, or principles, as implemented within the classroom environment ... later to be implemented in society ... in the business world ... in the industrial world ... in the political world ... in the social world!

While some theoreticians, in yet a different educational environment, think **students should be allowed to choose what** they want to learn ... and **when** they want to learn it, how many of us ... at a younger age would have freely chosen broccoli over ice cream ... self-discipline over doing what we wanted? How many students do you think would freely choose a well-rounded, balanced curriculum, let alone know how to implement such? As students' educational futures are planned at **Lahr-Well Academy,** we take into consideration the curricular foundation of **what** will be taught, **when** it will be taught, and **how** it will be taught!

Within U.S. "traditional" education, decades of proven, diminishing educational results ... alongside **increased "carte-blanche" federal and state funding ... without accountability** ... have **virtually destroyed "traditional" education (and generations of children within it), but** the teaching of **anti-patriotism** ... to the extent of **teaching students to "hate" the United States** ... **has sabotaged** U.S. education (and our country) **causing a downward spiral from which we may never recover! If** we are to recover, we **must throw ourselves** into **a proven** process **now!**

With "time running out," business, industry, and the military must immediately "step up to the plate" to train their own future employees and armed services members. This can be accomplished through **leasing and implementing the Lahr-Well Curriculum Concept of Synergistic Academics!** Smaller schools, requiring less square footage, could be offered to employees' children or military service children as an **added fringe-benefit**. Parents could receive financial benefits, in the form of tuition-grants/ scholarships, plus have the peace of mind knowing their children would be physically located close to them ... in a secured environment. Students would receive the academic, social, and patriotic benefits of an amazing, exceptional education K4 through grade 12. These, of course, would be, literally, **"Prep" or Preparatory** Schools!

Businesses, industry, and/or the armed services could then use the last year or two of high-school to train their "future personnel" with their own programs, or these entities could bring the early graduates into the "field" as interns for one to two years ... as repayment for their education scholarships ... as well as a trial period of what might be accomplished professionally if these students were to stay in the the business/ industry or armed forces "hosting" entity.

ALMEDA M. LAHR-WELL, Ph.D.

CHAPTER XIII

Here is the Answer: Saving U.S. Educational Exceptionalism!

If you will recall President Ronald Reagan's **1983** National Commission on Excellence in Education produces introductory comments on American education in the form of *A Nation at Risk: The Imperative for Educational Reform*:

> This report is concerned with only one of the many causes and dimensions of the problem, but it is the one that undergirds American prosperity, security, and civility. We report to the American people that … the educational foundations of our society are presently being eroded by a rising tide of mediocrity that threatens our very future as a Nation and a people. **What was unimaginable a generation ago has begun to occur--others** (other nations) **are matching and surpassing our educational attainments.**
>
> **If an unfriendly foreign power had attempted to impose on America the mediocre educational performance that exists today, we might well have viewed it as an act of war.** As it stands, we have allowed this to happen to ourselves. We have even squandered the gains in student achievement made in the wake of the Sputnik challenge. Moreover, we have dismantled essential support systems which helped make those gains possible. **We have, in effect, been committing an act of unthinking, unilateral educational disarmament.** [68]

(This author's clarification and bolding)

On December 13, 1984, just one short year after the *Nation at Risk* Report, the National Council for Geographic Education **and** the Association of American Geographers produce the following report for public consumption. Located in the Washington, D.C. UPI Archives, the report is titled: **One-fifth of students can't find US on a map.**

The Report statistics are listed in black.	**L-WCC/SA** responses are in red.
• One-fifth of students can't find U.S. on a map.	• **All L-WCC** students ages 5-18 **can** find the U.S. on a map.
• About 20 percent of American students identified Brazil as the United States on a world map and another 20 percent could not find the United States at all, two geography organizations reported today.	• This is **not** the case with **L-WCC** students … who are yearly taught … from the age of 4 through 18 … the geographical location of the 190+ U.N. recognized countries, as well as their capitals; as well as the world's great mountain ranges; the largest, principal mountains; the great world deserts; as well as the *100 Natural Wonders of the World*.
• Among students in eight industrialized nations tested in geography, young Americans ranked fourth. • Association executive director Bob Aangeenbrug said the report appears to demonstrate 'widespread geography illiteracy' in the United States.	• This is **not** the case with **L-WCC** students … who, from age 4 through grade 12 … are annually instructed in achieving world-geography literacy.
• 'There is a huge number of children and adults who haven't a clue about the relationship between geography and history or geography and anything else,' he said. 'We now have a generation that has a limited capacity to put those things together.'	• This is **not** the case with **Lahr-Well Curriculum Concept** students, … who from K4 through grade 12 … are taught, weekly, about the relationship between geography and history … as well as the relationship among geography, world history, American history, the natural sciences, art, literature, philosophy, and foreign languages.

Aangeenbrug states:

• The report cites 1983 tests in geography, science and math that the Dallas Times-Herald administered to 12-year-olds in eight industrialized nations.

• The tests, developed for the newspaper by four prominent educators including a Nobel Prize-winning scientist, were given to sixth graders in the Dallas area and to sixth graders in Australia, Canada, Britain, France, Japan, Sweden and Switzerland.

• The Swedish students were ranked first in the geography test.

ALMEDA M. LAHR-WELL, Ph.D.

Aangeenbrug continues:

• In a recent college-level survey of global understanding by the Educational Testing Service of 3,000 American undergraduates, the median score was 42.9 out of a possible 101.	• This is **not** the case with the **L-WCC** … where world, and U.S. geography **have always been**, and **will always be**, an integral element of the L-W Curriculum Concept.
• Part of the problem is that teachers are not well educated in geography and, 'That is why we put together this report. This is to put ammunition in people's hands so that teaching institutions can start working to put geography in their own curriculums.'	• Teachers not being well-educated in geography is **not** the case with the **L-WCC.** Teachers weekly grade their students' world and/or U.S. geography assignments. This, of course, teaches, or "reaffirms" teachers' geographical knowledge.

Evaluating students of a similar time frame, the Department of Education finds in a study that, of 20 children born in 1983, six did not graduate from high school on time in 2001. Of the remaining 14 who did, 10 started college that fall, but only five had earned a bachelor's degree after five years.

And then--almost 30 years after the **1983** report's release–the "unimaginable" happens. Things were beginning to seem hopeless. The situation continues to deteriorate … as explained in statistics from **Delisle's** *Dumbing Down America* (2014). The U.S. crises in education **have only worsened,** and are critiqued by Delisle in his *Dumbing Down America.*

However, unbeknownst to the powers-that-be of U.S. Education, a solution to the U.S. educational crises had already appeared in **1985** … (just after the **1983** *Nation at Risk Report*). That solution was **(and is) the Lahr-Well Curriculum Concept of Synergistic Academics!** The solution offers a "whole new set" of educational statistics!

Delisle's 2014 critiques are in black.	The 1985 L-WCC of SA are in red.
• More than half of all gifted students do not match their tested ability in school performance.	• This is **not** the case with the **Lahr-Well Curriculum Concept of Synergistic Academics** where **most** academically-at-risk, learning-disabled, average, and gifted students meet, and often exceed, their tested abilities.
• More than 40% of high school students could not draw inferences from written material.	• This is **not** the case with the **Lahr-Well Curriculum Concept** where **all** academically-at-risk, learning-disabled, average, and gifted students are taught daily, from age 4 through 12th grade, how to draw inferences from written, oral, aural and kinesthetic materials.
• The majority of secondary school students had mastered 80% of the content of their textbooks *before* ever opening them for the school year.	• This is **not** the case with the **L-WCC** where **all** academically-at-risk, learning-disabled, average, and gifted students' **tailored** curriculum is a combination of foundational mastery, as well as daily introduction of new concepts from age 4 through 12th grade.
• School curricula, for the most part, focused on memorization and acquisition of **low-level** skills, not on problem solving and analysis. (This author's emphasis)	• This is **not** the case with the **L-WCC** where **all** academically-at-risk, learning disabled, average, and gifted students, while embracing memorization of **some** facts, focus on acquisition of **highest-level** skills, problem solving, analysis, and critical thinking.
• Teacher training is especially lacking in math, science, and foreign languages, as well as in programs that focus on methods of teaching gifted students.	• This is **not** the case with the **L-WCC** where qualified and specialized instructors teach their specialized subject areas in math, in science, in composition, and in 5 foreign languages to **all** students: academically-at-risk, learning-disabled, average, and gifted ... K4 through grade 12. Additional training is constantly undertaken in team-teaching ... demanded by the curriculum content and approach.

ALMEDA M. LAHR-WELL, Ph.D.

CHAPTER XIV

Myth Buster: True or False? "There's No Place Like" Lahr-Well Academy (of SA)

TRUE: "There's NO Place Like" Lahr-Well Academy of Synergistic Academics!!!

When someone asks about my curriculum … and I give them a brief description, it is not uncommon for that person to blurt out, "Oh, I know a school **just like yours** in … Colorado … New York … Arkansas … " **These people are WRONG!!**

First: The person has **absolutely no knowledge** of what my program actually is!

Second: To my knowledge, there is **NO program in the United States** that is **equal to** the comprehensive, intensive curriculum of the **Lahr-Well Curriculum Concept of Synergistic Academics**!

How can I make **such a bold statement?** Although there may be schools where **elements** of my curriculum might be taught, tell me **where will you find**:

- a school where **5 foreign languages are required of each** student (ages 4-18)

- a school where--**every year**--**all** those same students are **also** required to study:

    ○ biology

    ○ chemistry

    ○ earth science

    ○ physics

    ○ robotics and engineering

while at the same time being required … through critical thinking … to memorize and connect:

    ○ the Preamble to the *U.S. Constitution*

    ○ the Amendments to the *U.S. Constitution*

    ○ the *Gettysburg Address* … etc., etc., etc.!

while at the same time reading **years** beyond their chronological ages?

If you will recall, reading years beyond chronological age has not been a "feather" in U.S. education's hat since the 1950s when Rudolf **Flesch** wrote "Why Johnny Can't Read." Now seven decades later--unlike students from **Lahr-Well Academy**--many Johnnys and Janies, of the U.S. "traditional," education system, **still** cannot read **at**, let alone **above**, their grade levels nor can they add, subtract, multiply, divide, or make change … without the assistance of a calculator or cash register! If you find that difficult to believe, just check with some of the local HR offices in your town or city!

Overwhelmingly, neither "traditional" high school nor college graduates "have a clue" of how to write a check … let alone how to prepare a budget. They have not been instructed in how to begin investing as soon as they earn their first dollars, or how to (or the need to) avoid debt. They haven't been warned about the pitfalls of "investing in their futures via college debt, or a new car (with all the frills), or the "American dream home" before they have a financially-secure position from which to do these things. And, although they can "master" levels of electronic games, and proficiently use social media "in their sleep," **can** they, and **will they**--with intellectual competence and critical-thinking abilities--**be able to be the problem solvers** of the **twenty-first century**? **Will they be able to** help keep the United States in a position equal to (or excelling beyond) other world powers … **if for no other reason than national security**? **Will they be able to** fill the need of cyber-security (aka information technology security) which protects computer systems, their networks, programs, devices and data from unauthorized access, attack, or damage? **Will they be able to** fill the professional positions in science, math, and technology of the future with the skill sets of today, or will **U.S. business and industry be forced to continue to reach out to other nations** to find **qualified candidates**? **Will they even know how to** present an idea or a product … or worse yet, **how to** "hold a face-to-face" conversation with another person in a business/industry transaction?

Lahr-Well Curriculum Concept students **do not and will not** have these deficiencies. **L-WCC** students have an exceptional, education foundation. The individual and inter-personal skills … lacking in so many of our U.S. "traditional" high school and college graduates … are part of the daily training for **L-WCC/SA** students where they are provided a prodigious educational foundation which includes: reinstating **conventional … long-established American values** through a specialized, "Renaissance" integrated and interdisciplinary academic curriculum … combined with a technology curriculum for K4 through grade 12 … (advancing from a quarter … 9 weeks … of typing, to a quarter of basic computer programs: Word, Excel, Power Point, as well as Google Docs, Google Sheets, Google Slides, to a quarter of coding, to a beginning program for Cyber-Security). **Every** student takes **every one of these subjects every year**, reviews the basics of each … **each** year … and then progresses annually to more advanced levels in **each of these subjects.** With **the Lahr-Well Curriculum Concept, every** student is being prepared to be a future local, national and/or global leader!

For many a disbeliever … who actually knows nothing of the Curriculum Concept … nothing of the implementation … nothing of the academic achievements … nothing of the "student-product" this seems **"impossible … unimaginable."** However, when statistics are presented, and students demonstrate their advanced expertise--in so many subjects, **the impossible becomes possible … the unimaginable becomes imaginable!**

ALMEDA M. LAHR-WELL, Ph.D.

(This is impossible with classrooms of more than 15 students!) Class sizes are limited to a maximum of 10 to 15 students **because** this is what helps students **become amazingly successful!** This could build to 10 subgroups of 55 students: 10 in Level I (K4 through 1st grade); 15 in Level II (2nd through 5th grades); 15 in Level III (6th through 8th grades); and 15 in Level IV (9th through 12th grades). The ideal maximum of student clientele in one building is estimated to be no more than 550 students … so that the administrator and the rest of the teaching-team know **every** student! The **bottom line here is student academic (and social) success!** (Sports and other interests can be met through community resources.)

There's NO place like Lahr-Well Academy!!!

CHAPTER XV

Conclusion: In Every Life There Are Defining Moments! This is One of Them!

For Such A Time As This!

If you did not know before, you know now the serious crises that face our country regarding education. "Traditional" methods in public, parochial and private schools are too often dictated by too many outdated, ineffective programs that **not only do not work**, but that also teach anti-intellectualism and anti-patriotism! **The L-WCC/SA is** a **proven** answer to these crises.

As stated before, too many "traditional" students are testing **years-behind** their chronological ages and, being frustrated and angry, are dropping out of school before graduation. They see no value or are unhappy in the "traditional" environment. Statistics show that students are learning less and less each decade, causing them to be unprepared and incapable of meeting the demands for college or university classes ... or for the jobs of today and tomorrow. **Too many highly-trained and qualified educators are discouraged** with the "traditional" system and are leaving ... **dropping out of** ... the U.S. teaching force ... frequently after just 5 years or less! I have personally witnessed this mass-exodus in my last 2-3 decades of teaching. This is a formula for, yet, a greater disaster to come!

With the **L-WCC, students enjoy** coming to school! They enthusiastically embrace the academic challenges, and find the classwork worthwhile, and the daily science experiments and/or activities, and monthly field trips exciting. The teachers, while challenged to prepare work for students on an individual (**and** class) basis, instead of continually teaching the "one-size-fits-all" curriculum, work together as a team, and find their efforts rewarding, especially when they see advanced, student-results **and** well-adjusted students!

Every child **deserves** this kind of education ... in a small classroom environment with "one-on-one" teacher attention ... enhanced by class projects, daily science activities and/or experiments, tailored computer instruction in language arts and math, tailored classroom instruction in basic skills, class instruction in the social sciences, art, music history and foreign languages. Daily **oral, aural, visual and kinesthetic** methods reach **every** child ... at one point or another!

Every educator **deserves** an environment where he/she can reach **every** child in **every** subject! Teachers **deserve** to work as a team … reinforced by their colleagues and their administrator. Teachers **deserve** an environment where **every** parent is involved … to a certain extent … with the team-approach to student success!

This is what happens at **Lahr-Well Academy** with **the Lahr-Well Curriculum Concept of Synergistic Academics**! **This** is what **should happen** in every U.S. classroom! **This** is the information I want to share with educators, business, industry, and the military throughout the country. I **know** what this **Curriculum** … when implemented correctly … **can do** for **every** child! There are **nationally-standardized test results … as well as documented student performance** of what it has done for **Lahr-Well Academy** students … academically-at-risk, learning-disabled, average, and gifted!

What happens at Lahr-Well Academy … Changes Students' Lives!!!

After reading this book, you now know what **the Lahr-Well Curriculum Concept of Synergistic Academics** offers: **exceptional, comprehensive, intensive academics; "conventional" ethics; integrity and patriotism** … basically, one of the best … if not **the best** … programs in the nation! Actually, **the Concept** could be established **anywhere** in the United States … or abroad … and students would be able to transfer, to the same program, in October, January, or March … and "not miss a beat"! (Speaking of **beats** … hence, for me, it is similar in concept to the Suzuki Music Program.)

"Now is the time for all good men (and women) to come to the aid of their" … **children, grandchildren, great grandchildren … of the "future" of the United States! Now is the time for YOU to DO SOMETHING!**

Credited to Sir Winston Churchill are the words: "**Men** (people) **occasionally stumble over the truth, but most of them pick themselves up and hurry off as if nothing ever happened.**" These words address so many issues in our lives, but none quite so urgent as that of the U.S. educational system crises. **Now** is **not** the time for you to be one of those men (or people) to whom Winston Churchill refers!

Put into other words, perhaps, we should also reflect on an observation of the famous, fictitious character of 1605: Don Quixote de la Mancha, a middle-aged "hidalgo" (gentleman) from Spain, obsessed with chivalrous ideals. He takes up lance and sword (as did the knights of the Middle Ages) **to defend the helpless and destroy the wicked**. In our time … portrayed as a "madman" (which I do not think he was … or is) he "spouts off" (in the musical version *Man of La Mancha*), about sanity and madness … saying, "and the maddest of all … to see life as it is and not as it should be"! So, why do the U.S. education system **and** American society insist on seeing and accepting "what is," instead of **defending** the "helpless" children … by "making their reality … not what it is, but rather **what it should be**"?

Hidden in the recesses of the U.S. Midwest is a private K4 through grade 12 Academy that has made U.S. education **what it should be** for almost 4 decades! It has **not abandoned** our country's **"conventional" long-ago established values,** but has, indeed, **embodied and emboldened** our country's heritage along with embracing foundational skills, multi-languages, the natural and social sciences, technological training, as well as independent and creative/critical thinking. **Here is a story to tell to the nation/s!**

Administrators and teachers need to know that this will work for them. It won't take much more time, and it **should** take less money than "traditional" education is now spending … per student … on ineffective programs. Teachers will probably enjoy this method much more than what they are now doing. Students are more actively engaged in daily learning. They have fun in the classroom, and learn far more than with the antiquated, "traditional," anti-American methods.

The Lahr-Well Curriculum Concept of Synergistic Academics is patented and can be licensed through me. I created and designed the Curriculum, and have spent the last 35 years, with the aid of my Academy teachers, in research and development … fine-tuning every aspect of the program. All administrators and educators are required to spend a one-year internship at the Academy studying the pedagogy and implementation of the Curriculum, as well as learning how to meet the needs of every student, in addition to learning how to always function as a teaching-team member.

I invite you to come witness this **exceptional** program, the **exceptional** staff, the **exceptional** students and their **exceptional** academic achievements. **The Lahr-Well Curriculum Concept of Synergistic Academics** could be duplicated throughout the United States … **restoring** our long-ago established **"conventional" American values and our highly-valued educational leadership … giving to the American people the academic standards, insights, and values every student in the United States deserves!**

The L-WCC is a non-graded curriculum. The student body is composed of students of varied racial, ethnic, economic, and religious backgrounds. The **Curriculum** accommodates students moving at different paces in different basic skills subjects. This **freedom** … "across the board" … as comprehensive and intensive as it is, is almost unheard of in most U.S. "traditional," parochial, and many private schools. Generally, the theory is rejected by "traditional" education … whether that be elementary and/or secondary schools … or university and college education departments!

With **the Lahr-Well Curriculum Concept of Synergistic Academics**, teachers have to work a little "harder" to "keep up with" the different nuances, but the challenges are edifying, and **the student academic-achievement, as well as the relaxed, but disciplined classroom-environment … and collegial team-work are powerful!**

"Traditional" classes are not structured (time-wise nor ability-wise) to allow for this kind of individualization … this **tailoring** of curriculum. Class "instruction" times average 25-45 minutes. **The Curriculum Concept** divides students into 4 levels: Level I is prekindergarten (K4) through 1st grade. Level II is 2nd through 5th grades. Level III is 6th through 8th grades. Level IV is 9th through 12th grades. Students work well together in this cross-grade-level environment. This allows for older students to reinforce the academic material (for themselves, as well as the younger students); allows the older students to mentor the younger students … as the older students learn more patience, more understanding, and more tolerance of younger students; and allows for younger students to "set their sights on" the academic accomplishments of the "upper classmen." Of course, teachers always have to be attentive to … and "guarded about" … the social interactions of differing ages; but the **L-WCC** staff is trained to constantly observe and to immediately respond.

ALMEDA M. LAHR-WELL, Ph.D.

There will be those who will immediately say, "This won't work for us!" However, the only reason it wouldn't work is that naysayers don't **want** it to work … because **Lahr-Well Academy** has 35 years of nationally, standardized test scores, that **prove it does work!**

Now, in the first quarter of the 21st century, the "state of education crises" is still a "hot topic" of debate because reading, math and science scores are **still weak and still declining**. This doesn't even take into consideration the **lack of composition skills** of K4 through grade 12 students, nor **the absence of** critical/creative thinking, nor **non-existent** foreign languages, **nor sabotaged** American history! There are those who want to "throw out" the education of the **early** 20th century as a thing of the past … worthy of no merit. **However, the Lahr-Well Curriculum Concept of Synergistic Academics is built on the meritorious concepts of the early U.S. 20th century,** and actually discards the ineffective education trends, fashions, fads, and dogmas of the latter part of the 20th century while yet embracing the technology of the 21st.

On one hand, where we in the United States landed **at the end** of the 20th century **is not the global stronghold** we held **at the beginning of the 20th. In the 21st century we, as a nation, must reestablish our strength … matched with local, national and global compassion**. In achieving this, **we cannot afford to continue to teach our students to "hate" the United States. Nor can we afford to lose more of our future (students) as we watch test scores in reading, math, science, composition and American history continue to "spiral downward"!**

Graduates of **Lahr-Well Academy are** well-rounded, academically superior, patriotic problem-solvers ready to tackle the world as mature, responsible, critical/creative thinking adults! **The Curriculum** solves the problems of the academic shortfalls, as well as anti-patriotism. **The Curriculum** gives teachers, students, and parents **what students need to excel** … to excel academically, to excel socially, to excel as responsible adults, to excel as patriotic citizens.

In addition to the academic, intellectual and patriotic assets, **the Curriculum** provides students with an enhanced knowledge and understanding of **what** our government **is and how** it works. **L-WCC** students--being "schooled" in the benefits as well as the shortcomings--of Capitalism, Socialism, Marxism and Communism eventually understand the freedoms and liberties that **only one** of these systems offers. Students are taught to **value the good** in the United States, to work to eliminate the bad, and to continue to make it a country **respectful** of **all**. Students are encouraged to view the United States … not as an "evil victimizing-empire," but rather credited as **the country** … though admittedly flawed … **that has brought democracy to more people in the world … than has any other nation in history!**

Students are taught how to analyze and **how to help make** their homelife, their community, their country, and their world **better places** for **all.** When students are **not taught** what they need to know … when **"they don't know what they don't know"** … about their *Constitution,* Amendments, their civil rights and liberties **and basic academics … they remain ignorant. Their ignorance** leaves them **vulnerable** to **indoctrination**! Their indoctrination leaves them vulnerable to **losing** their **country, their freedom and their liberties**!

L-WCC students are taught that if they see something they think needs to be changed … they **must** become **proactive in offering a better solution**--not a destructive solution--a positive solution that will bring about desired changes … **for the betterment of all**.

For the past 70 years "traditional" education has told us that it has been *trying* to bring about positive solutions to our U.S. education crises. However, trend after trend, fashion after fashion, fad after fad … billions after billions of dollars … have been "thrown against the wall … to see what sticks" while test scores have continued to plummet! Added to these **failed efforts … and more generations of students lost** … has been the intentional indoctrination to destroy the foundation of the "American Way of Life" and its family values, American, Judeo-Christian values, American Exceptionalism and American Patriotism … to the extent that they have all but disappeared!

The **Lahr-Well Curriculum Concept of Synergistic Academics** not only offers **proven solutions to these education crises**, it **boldly reaffirms** the **"conventional" American, patriotic values of generations past … restoring** our long-ago established American values and our exceptional educational leadership … giving to the American people the academic standards, insights, and values every student in the United States deserves!

YOU MAY SAY, "THIS IS IMPOSSIBLE!" … BUT YOU NEED TO

VISIT THE ACADEMY TO ACTUALLY SEE IT IN ACTION!

ALMEDA M. LAHR-WELL, Ph.D.

ENDNOTES

1   Flesch, *Why Johnny Can't Read.*

2   Sowell, *Inside American Education*, 89

3   Ibid., 89-90

4   Ibid., 90-91

5   *A Nation At Risk Report*

6   Sowell, *IAE*, jacket cover

7   Ibid.

8   Ibid., 247

9   Ibid.

10 Ibid., 256

11 Ibid., ix

12 Ibid., 6

13 Ibid., 7

14 Ibid., 2

15 Ibid.

16 Ibid.

17 Weller, *Business Insider*

18 Sowell, *IAE*, 3

19 Ibid., 285

20 Ibid.

21 Ibid., 17

22 Ibid., 99

23 Sykes, *Dumbing Down Our Kids*, flapcover

24 Ibid., flapcover

25 Ibid.

26 Hearne, *Long War and Common Core*, xii

27 Delisle, *Dumbing Down America*, 103

28 Ibid., 105

29 Ibid., 107-108

30 Ibid., ix

31 Ibid., x

32 Ibid., xi

33 Ibid.

34 Ibid., xii

35 Spelling, *A National Accountable.,*1

36 Delisle, *DDA*, 94.

37 Ibid., 38

38 Ibid.

39 Ibid., 39

40 Ibid., 40

41 Ibid., 56

42 Ibid., 94

43 Ibid., 96

44 Ibid., 97

45 Ibid., 98

46 Ibid., 99

47 Ibid., 11

48 Hearne, *The Long War and Common Core*, xiv

49 Ibid., 3

50 Ibid., 4

51 Ibid., 6

52 Ibid., 4

53 Ibid., 5

54 Ibid.

55 Ibid.

56 Ibid.

57 Ibid., 34

58 Ibid., 36

59 Ibid.

60 Zinn, *A People's History*, flap cover

61 Ibid., 171

62 Ibid. 677-678

63 Hearne, *The LW*, xiii

64 Ibid.,35

65 Ibid.

66 Ibid., xvi

67 *A Nation At Risk*, 1983

68 Ibid.

WORKS CITED

Accountability Works. *National Cost of Aligning States and Localities to the Common Core Standards: A Pioneer Institute and American Principles Project White Paper (#82)*. Feb. 2012.

Common Core State Standards Initiative. "English Language Arts Standards." *Corestandards.Org*, 2019, www.corestandards.org/ELA-Literacy/.

---. "Read the Standards." *Corestandards.Org*, 2018, www.corestandards.org/read-the-standards/.

Cooperative Institutional Research Program. *The American Freshman: National Norms for Fall 1989*. The Higher Education Research Institution, UCLA, 1989.

---. *The American Freshman: National Norms for Fall 1990*. The Higher Education Research Institution, UCLA, 1990.

Delisle, James R. *Dumbing down America: The War on Our Nation's Brightest Young Minds (and What We Can Do to Fight Back)*. Waco, Texas, Prufrock Press, Inc, 2014.

Divounguy, Orphe, et al. "Illinois Wastes Millions of Education Dollars on Unnecessary Layers of Administration." *Illinois Policy*, 9 Sept. 2019, www.illinoispolicy.org/reports/bureaucrats-over-classrooms-illinois-wastes-millions-of-education-dollars-on-unnecessary-layers-of-administration/.

Flesch, Rudolf. *Why Johnny Can't Read: And What You Can Do about It*. New York, Harper & Row, 1955.

Hearne, Donna H. *The Long War and Common Core: & Everything You Need to Know to Win the War!* St. Louis, MO, Freedom Basics Press, 2015.

Hill, Bryce, and Joe Tabor. "Illinois Spends More on Education, but Outcomes Lag." *Illinois Policy*, 25 Feb. 2018, www.illinoispolicy.org/illinois-spends-more-on-education-but-outcomes-lag/.

Hobbs, Tawnell D. "SAT Scores Fall as More Students Take the Test." *Wall Street Journal*, 24 Sept. 2019.

"Illiteracy in America: Troubling Statistics and How Schools Can Help." *ResilientEducator.Com*, 5 Mar. 2018, resilienteducator.com/news/illiteracy-in-america/.

Minnicino, Michael. "The New Dark Age, The Frankfurt School and 'Political Correctness.'" *Fidelio Magazine*, 1992.

National Commission on Education. *A Nation at Risk Report*. U.S. Dept. of Education, 1983.

National Commission on Language Learning in the United States. *America's Languages: Investing in Language Education for the 21st Century*. American Academy of Arts and Sciences, 2017.

Pullmann, Joy. "Common Core Costs CA Nearly $10 Billion; Nation $80 Billion." *The Federalist*, 27 Jan. 2016, thefederalist.com/2016/01/27/estimate-common-core-to-cost-california-nearly-10-billion-nation-80-billion/.

Ripley, Amanda. "The Case Against High-School Sports." *The Atlantic*, Oct. 2013.

Silberman, Charles E. *Crisis in the Classroom; the Remaking of American Education.* New York, Vintage Books, 1970.

Sowell, Thomas. *Inside American Education: The Decline, the Deception, the Dogmas.* New York, Free Press, 1993.

Stossel, John. *Stupid in America: Are Our Kids Being Cheated out of a Good Education?* ABC, 13 Jan. 2006. Newscast.

Strauss, Karsten. "These Are the Skills Bosses Say New College Grads Do Not Have." *Forbes,* 17 May 2016.

Sykes, Charles J. *Dumbing down Our Kids: Why America's Children Feel Good about Themselves but Can't Read, Write, or Add.* New York, St. Martin's Press, 1995.

Thomas More Law Center. "Thomas More Law Center | The Sword and Shield for People of Faith." *Thomas More Law Center,* www.thomasmore.org/. Accessed 15 Apr. 2019.

U.S. Department of Commerce. "U.S. Bureau of Economic Analysis (BEA)." *Bea.Gov,* 2000, www.bea.gov/.

U.S. Department of Education. *A Nation Accountable: Twenty-Five Years after A Nation at Risk.* 2008.

Weller, Chris. "There's a New Path to Harvard and It's Not in a Classroom." *Business Insider,* 3 Sept. 2015.

Zinn, Howard. *A People's History of the United States.* New York, Harper Collins, 2015.